MW00769362

Crystallization-Study
of
Isaiah

Volume One

Witness Lee

The Holy Word for Morning Revival

Living Stream Ministry
Anaheim, CA • www.lsm.org

First Edition, July 2010.

ISBN 978-0-7363-4401-2

Published by

Living Stream Ministry
2431 W. La Palma Ave., Anaheim, CA 92801 U.S.A.
P. O. Box 2121, Anaheim, CA 92814 U.S.A.

Printed in the United States of America

10 11 12 13 14 / 6 5 4 3 2 1

Contents

Preface

1. This book is intended as an aid to believers in developing a daily time of morning revival with the Lord in His word. At the same time, it provides a limited review of the summer training held June 28—July 3, 2010, in Anaheim, California, on the "Crystallization-study of Isaiah." Through intimate contact with the Lord in His word, the believers can be constituted with life and truth and thereby equipped to prophesy in the meetings of the church unto the building up of the Body of Christ.

2. The entire content of this book is taken from the *Crystallization-study Outlines: Isaiah (1),* the text and footnotes of the Recovery Version of the Bible, selections from the writings of Witness Lee and Watchman Nee, and *Hymns,* all of which are published by Living Stream Ministry.

3. The book is divided into weeks. One training message is covered per week. Each week presents first the message outline, followed by six daily portions, a hymn, and then some space for writing. The training outline has been divided into days, corresponding to the six daily portions. Each daily portion covers certain points and begins with a section entitled "Morning Nourishment." This section contains selected verses and a short reading that can provide rich spiritual nourishment through intimate fellowship with the Lord. The "Morning Nourishment" is followed by a section entitled "Today's Reading," a longer portion of ministry related to the day's main points. Each day's portion concludes with a short list of references for further reading and some space for the saints to make notes concerning their spiritual inspiration, enlightenment, and enjoyment to serve as a reminder of what they have received of the Lord that day.

4. The space provided at the end of each week is for composing a short prophecy. This prophecy can be composed by considering all of our daily notes, the "harvest" of our inspirations during the week, and preparing a main point

with some sub-points to be spoken in the church meetings for the organic building up of the Body of Christ.

5. Following the last week in this volume, we have provided reading schedules for both the Old and New Testaments in the Recovery Version with footnotes. These schedules are arranged so that one can read through both the Old and New Testaments of the Recovery Version with footnotes in two years.

6. As a practical aid to the saints' feeding on the Word throughout the day, we have provided verse cards at the end of the volume, which correspond to each day's scripture reading. These may be cut out and carried along as a source of spiritual enlightenment and nourishment in the saints' daily lives.

7. The *Crystallization-study Outlines: Isaiah (1)* were compiled by Living Stream Ministry from the writings of Witness Lee and Watchman Nee. The outlines, footnotes, and cross-references in the Recovery Version of the Bible are by Witness Lee. All of the other references cited in this publication are from the published ministry of Witness Lee and Watchman Nee.

Summer Training
(June 28—July 3, 2010)

CRYSTALLIZATION-STUDY
OF ISAIAH

Banners:

The Christ who was processed
for the divine purposes
is the centrality and universality
of the great wheel of the move of the Divine Trinity
for the accomplishing of His economy
in the divine dispensing of Himself into His elect.

The Lord Jehovah—the eternal Triune God
who reveals Himself by speaking—
is our Husband, our salvation, and our living water,
and He desires to have a dwelling place
in which God is built into man and man is built into God.

We need to enjoy Christ as the sprout
and the branch to grow in Christ
and as the banner and the standard
to propagate Christ in the principle of the restoration of life
for a new revival.

Immanuel, the all-inclusive Christ—
the Shoot of Jehovah, the Fruit of the earth,
the Wonderful Counselor, the Mighty God,
the Eternal Father, the Prince of Peace, the great light—
is the universal replacement
so that He might become everything in God's economy.

Christ is a crown of glory and a diadem of beauty
for the reward of the overcomers;
a foundation, a tested stone, and
a precious cornerstone for the building of God;
and a supplying, caring, and covering King
for the kingdom of God.

The all-inclusive Christ—the King who will reign
in the tent of David in the coming age of restoration—
is now the King reigning over us
in the kingdom of the Son of God's love
by feeding us with Himself as the all-inclusive bread.

The Vision, the Word, and the Burden That Isaiah Saw concerning Christ as the Centrality and Universality of God's Eternal Economy

Scripture Reading: Isa. 1:1; 2:1; 13:1; 9:6-7; 40:28-31; 42:1-4; 53:5; 55:6-13; 57:15; 66:1-2

Day 1

IN the book of Ezekiel God's economy God's move in His economy are signified by a wheel.

I. Isaiah (meaning "the salvation of Jah") is the leading book among all the books of the prophets, and its subject is the salvation of Jehovah through the incarnated, crucified, resurrected, ascended, and coming Christ; this book is the vision that Isaiah saw (1:1), the word that Isaiah saw (2:1), and the burden that Isaiah saw (13:1; 15:1) concerning Christ as the centrality and universality of God's eternal economy (9:6-7; 53:1-12; 40:10):

A. Isaiah reveals the history of the universe—from God's original creation through Satan's rebellion and Christ's processes to accomplish God's judicial redemption and His organic salvation for the producing and building up of the Body of Christ, to usher in the kingdom of God unto the New Jerusalem in the new heaven and new earth (v. 22a; 45:18; 14:12-14; 53:5; 12:2-3; 65:17).

B. Isaiah's prophecy has a spiritual essence—the Christ who was processed for the divine purposes is the centrality and universality of the great wheel of the move of the Divine Trinity for the accomplishing of His economy in the divine dispensing of Himself into His elect (cf. Ezek. 1:15).

Day 2

II. In the book of Isaiah, God's love toward Israel is exercised in a threefold way: as a Father (1:2-3; 63:16; 64:8), as a nursing Mother (66:12-13), and as a Husband (54:5):

A. God deals with people according to what He is; as the Holy One (1:4), He chastises His people that they may be holy (Heb. 12:10), and as the

righteous One (Isa. 24:16a), He judges the nations
because they are not just and righteous (26:13).

B. God's dealing in love with His beloved Israel
and His righteous judgment upon the nations
bring in Christ, the Savior (43:3-4; 49:26).

C. There is a divine, spiritual, and heavenly philosophy that dominates the book of Isaiah:

1. God's chastising of Israel and His judgment
on the nations who exercise excessive action
upon Israel issue in three things:

   a. Israel is brought back to God.
   b. The created things are restored.
   c. The all-inclusive Christ is ushered in.

2. When Israel turns to God, there will be the
restoration of all things, and then the all-
inclusive Christ will be ushered in; this is
the divine, spiritual, and heavenly philosophy that dominates the book of Isaiah,
especially in the first thirty-nine chapters.

Day 3 III. **The book of Isaiah, which has sixty-six chapters, is a representative of the entire Bible, which has sixty-six books:**

A. The first section (chs. 1—39) concerns God's
governmental dealing with His beloved Israel
and His punishing judgment on the nations so
that Israel may be brought back to God and the
all-inclusive Christ may be ushered in with the
expected restoration of all things (11:6-9; 35:5-6;
cf. Matt. 19:28).

B. The last section (Isa. 40—66) is the kind word
of Jehovah spoken to the heart of Israel, His
beloved people; this word unveils the prophet's
vision concerning the redeeming and saving
Christ as the Servant of Jehovah and reveals
the all-inclusive salvation brought in by Christ
to Israel and the nations, with the full restoration of all things, consummating in the new
heaven and new earth.

IV. **The book of Isaiah reveals the Triune God**

coming out of eternity into time and with His divinity into humanity to pass through the processes of incarnation, human living, crucifixion, resurrection, and ascension for the accomplishment of God's economy to produce and build up the church as the Body of Christ and to usher in the kingdom age, consummating in the New Jerusalem in the new heaven and new earth:

A. Isaiah reveals the forerunner of Christ, preparing the way for Christ (40:1-5).

B. Isaiah reveals the conception and birth of Christ as the embodiment of the Triune God (7:14; 9:6-7).

C. Isaiah reveals the human living of Christ (7:14-15; 40:9b; 53:2-3; 61:1-2a; 9:2; 49:5a; 42:1-4; 11:1-2).

D. Isaiah reveals the crucifixion of Christ (53:4-10a, 12b).

E. Isaiah reveals the resurrection of Christ (vv. 10b-11).

F. Isaiah reveals the ascension of Christ (52:13; 53:12a).

G. Isaiah reveals the second coming of Christ (40:10; 64:1).

H. Isaiah reveals the coming kingdom of Christ (2:2-5; 11:6-9; 35:1-10; 30:26).

I. Isaiah reveals the eternal new creation of Christ (65:17).

Day 4 **V. Isaiah reveals the wonderful person of Christ:**

A. Christ is the incarnated Savior, the crucified Redeemer, the resurrected Life-giver, the ascended Victor, and the coming King (9:6; 53:5, 10b-12; 40:10).

B. Christ is the light of Jehovah (2:5; 9:1-2; 49:6b).

C. Christ is the Shoot of Jehovah and the Fruit of the earth (4:2).

D. Christ is the King, Jehovah of hosts (6:1-8).

E. Christ is God with us (7:14; 8:8, 10; 40:9b).

F. Christ is Wonderful (9:6).

G. Christ is our Counselor (v. 6).

H. Christ is the Mighty God and the Eternal Father (v. 6).

    I. Christ is the Prince of Peace (v. 6).

    J. Christ is our sanctuary, our dwelling place (8:14a).

    K. Christ is the branch from the roots of Jesse, the father of David (11:1-9).

    L. Christ is a banner to the peoples and a standard to the nations (vv. 10-16).

    M. Christ is the springs of salvation, the salvation of Jehovah (12:2-6).

    N. Christ as our King is our eternal rock, our Savior, Defender, and Teacher (16:5; 24:23; 26:3-4; 17:10; 30:29; 19:20; 30:20-21).

    O. Christ is the Steward in the house of God, the One who has the key of the house of David (22:15, 20-24; Rev. 3:7).

    P. Christ is a peg, a nail, driven into a sure place (Isa. 22:23).

    Q. Christ is our crown of glory and our diadem of beauty (28:5).

    R. Christ is the foundation and cornerstone of God's building (v. 16).

    S. Christ is a refuge from the wind, a covering from the tempest, streams of water in a dry place, and the shadow of a massive rock in a wasted land (32:2).

    T. Christ is the arm of Jehovah (53:1).

    U. Christ is our Husband (54:5-7).

    V. Christ is a man of sorrows in His humanity to be our Redeemer (53:3).

    W. Christ is the sure mercies shown to David (55:3).

    X. Christ is a Witness, a Leader, and a Commander to the peoples (v. 4).

    Y. Christ is our refuge, our land, and our holy mountain (57:13b).

    Z. Christ is the Angel of Jehovah, the Angel of His presence (63:9).

Day 5 **VI. Isaiah speaks of God's building as the goal of God; the church with its ultimate manifestation, the New Jerusalem, is the house of Jehovah's beauty (1 Cor. 3:9, 12a; Rev. 21:3, 18-22; Psa. 27:4):**

A. The house of Jehovah as His dwelling place is the mingling and the mutual abode of God and man (Isa. 57:15; 66:1-2; John 14:2, 20, 23; 15:4; 1 John 4:13).
B. "I will beautify the house of My beauty"—God beautifies us by dispensing Himself into us (Isa. 60:7b).
C. "Jehovah your God /...The Holy One of Israel...He has beautified you" (v. 9c).
D. "To beautify the place of My sanctuary; / And I will make the place for My feet glorious" (v. 13b).
E. "Jehovah will be an eternal light to you, / And your God your beauty" (v. 19b):
   1. As the New Jerusalem we will enjoy Jehovah in Christ, the Servant of Jehovah, as the eternal light (vv. 19-20; Rev. 21:23; 22:5).
   2. In the restoration God in Christ will be our glory and beauty, and we will be Christ's glory and beauty; thus, God and His chosen people will be glorified and beautified in mutuality (Isa. 60:21; 61:3b; Eph. 3:21; cf. Exo. 28:2).
   3. This will be accomplished by the divine dispensing through Christ as the Redeemer and the Savior putting Himself, as the life-giving Spirit and the word, into God's people (Isa. 59:21; Eph. 5:26-27; S. S. 1:10-11).

Day 6 VII. **Isaiah speaks of the enjoyment of Christ for God's building:**
A. We need to see a revelation of our fallen condition and the revelation of Christ in glory (Isa. 1:18; 57:20-21; 64:6-8; 6:1-8).
B. We need to keep our hearts turned to the Lord to be saved from hypocrisy (29:13; 45:22).
C. We need to be infused with the Lord as our life power and multiplied strength (40:28-31; 12:2-4).
D. We need to seek Jehovah and return to Him and His word as the rain and snow for the renewing of our mind with His thoughts and ways (55:6-13).
E. We need to have a contrite and lowly spirit (57:15; 66:2).

    F. We need to trust in the name of Jehovah and rely on our God (50:10-11).

    G. We need to enjoy the Lord as the depths of God by loving Him with Him as our love (49:15-16; 64:3-4; 1 Cor. 2:9).

VIII. Isaiah speaks of our service in Christ for God's building:

    A. We need to be watchmen on the walls of Jerusalem, making the church a house of prayer (Isa. 62:6-7; 56:7).

    B. We need to be one with Christ as His disciples to speak and hear as instructed ones (50:4-5).

    C. We need to be one with Christ to proclaim the jubilee of grace (61:1-2; 49:6).

    D. We need to be one with Christ as nursing mothers to shepherd God's people (vv. 14-16; 66:12-13; 42:3; 1 Thes. 2:7-8).

Morning Nourishment

Isa. The vision of Isaiah the son of Amoz, which he saw
1:1 concerning Judah and Jerusalem...
9:6-7 For a child is born to us, a Son is given to us; and the
government is upon His shoulder; and His name will
be called Wonderful Counselor, Mighty God, Eternal
Father, Prince of Peace. To the increase of *His* government and to *His* peace there is no end, upon the
throne of David and over His kingdom, to establish it
and to uphold it in justice and righteousness from
now to eternity. The zeal of Jehovah of hosts will
accomplish this.

Isaiah's prophecy has a spiritual essence, and the essence is
this: The Christ processed for the divine purposes being the centrality and the universality of the great wheel of the move of the
Divine Trinity for the divine dispensing of Himself into His elect.
Although the term *great wheel* cannot be found in Isaiah, this
book does in fact speak of the great wheel of the move of the
Divine Trinity. Each of the books of prophecy unveils a part of
God's universal move. Whereas Ezekiel uses the word *wheel* to
describe God's universal move on earth for the fulfillment of His
eternal economy (Ezek. 1:15), Isaiah takes the lead to prophesy
concerning God's move.

The book of Isaiah is full of the aspects of God's eternal economy. This book shows us how God, for the fulfillment of His eternal economy, has chosen a people, Israel, to be His elect and His
beloved. Around Israel are the Gentile nations. In a sense, Israel
has been chosen by God, and the nations have been set aside by
Him. Nevertheless, in His move God cannot neglect the nations.
Therefore, both Israel, God's chosen and beloved people, and the
nations are very much involved in Isaiah's prophecy. (*Life-study of
Isaiah,* p. 1)

Today's Reading

The best way to study Isaiah is to learn the secret and mysterious points of this book. Many of these secret points are related to

Christ. Every aspect of what Christ is and of what He has done, is doing, and will do involves a secret. Some of these secrets are in Isaiah 7:14 and 9:6; others are in chapter fifty-three. In this book, there are secrets even concerning Babylon. When we get into all the secret and mysterious points in Isaiah, the whole book is open to us. (*Life-study of Isaiah,* p. 2)

[*Isaiah* means] *the salvation of Jah.* The book of Isaiah, in its content concerning God's eternal economy in Christ, is the leading book among all the books of the prophets. This book is the vision that Isaiah saw (Isa. 1:1), the word that Isaiah saw (2:1), and the burden that Isaiah saw (13:1; 15:1). The vision, word, and burden in Isaiah are concerned with God's eternal economy in Christ, which is thoroughly covered in this book.

The book of Isaiah unveils that God's dealing in love with His beloved Israel and His righteous judgment upon the nations bring in Christ, the Savior (43:3; 49:26), who is God (9:6) incarnated to be a man (7:14), possessing both the divine nature and the human nature (4:2), living on this earth (53:2-3; 42:1-4), crucified (53:7-10a, 12), resurrected (53:10b-11), ascended (52:13), and coming (40:10; 64:1) to meet the need of God's chosen people and the nations (9:1-7; 49:6) in God's all-inclusive salvation (12:2-3), that the restoration of all things, of the created yet fallen universe (2:2-5; 11:6-9; 35:1-10; 30:26), may be brought in, which will consummate in the new heaven and new earth for eternity (65:17). Hence, the content of Isaiah covers God's entire economy of the New Testament, from the incarnation (Matt. 1:18-25) to the new heaven and new earth (Rev. 21-22), with the Old Testament background of God's dealing with Israel and His judgment upon the nations. According to Isaiah's prophecy, the Christ who was processed for the divine purposes is the centrality and universality of the great wheel of the move of the Divine Trinity (Ezek. 1:15 and footnote 1) for the accomplishing of His economy in the divine dispensing of Himself into His elect. (Isa. 1:1, footnote 1)

Further Reading: Life-study of Isaiah, msg. 1

Enlightenment and inspiration: _____
_____
_____

Morning Nourishment

Isa. **For thus says Jehovah, I now am extending to her**
66:12-13 **peace like a river, and the glory of the nations like an**
overflowing stream; and you will nurse, you will be
carried on the hip, and you will be bounced on the
knees. As one whom his mother comforts, so will I com-
fort you; and you will be comforted in Jerusalem.
54:5 **For your Maker is your Husband; Jehovah of hosts is**
His name....

Both Israel and the nations, the Gentiles, are dealt with by God, but in different ways. God's dealing with Israel, His beloved people, is always in love. For this reason, I consider this dealing not as judgment but as chastisement. God's dealing with Israel is like a father's dealing with his children to correct them, to improve them, and to bring them onto the right track. This is chastisement.

In the book of Isaiah, God's love toward Israel is exercised in a threefold way, as a Father (1:2-3; 63:16; 64:8), as a nursing Mother (66:13), and as a Husband (54:5). God was Israel's Father, Mother, and Husband. Since God dealt with His beloved Israel in a loving way, His dealing with them was not a matter of judgment but of chastisement. (*Life-study of Isaiah,* p. 6)

Today's Reading

God's dealing with the nations, however, is a matter of judgment. This judgment is not based on God's love; it is based on God's righteousness, on His justice. When God comes to deal with people, He deals with them according to what He is. The Bible reveals that God is holy and righteous. He is the Holy One and the Righteous One. As the Holy One, He deals with His people, and as the Righteous One, He deals with the nations.

God deals with His elect in love that they may be holy. Because the children of Israel were called by God and separated unto God, they must be holy, as God is holy. God's chastisement of Israel was for holiness (Heb. 12:10). Since they had become common, worldly, and completely unlike God in His holy nature, He came in to chastise them...that they might learn the lessons of holiness and be holy.

God's dealing with the nations is different from His dealing with Israel. Whereas God chastises Israel according to His holiness, He judges the nations according to His righteousness. God judges the nations because they are not just and righteous. Therefore, based upon what God is in His righteousness, He comes in to judge the nations.

As we read the book of Isaiah, we need to keep in mind that God's dealing with people is in two aspects—the aspect of His holiness and the aspect of His righteousness. Holiness is God's requirement for His chosen people, and righteousness is God's requirement for the nations. God wants His people to be holy, and He wants the nations to be righteous. Based upon His holiness and righteousness, God deals respectively with these two classes of people. He chastises Israel in love for holiness, and He judges the nations for righteousness.

God's chastisement of Israel and His judgment upon the nations who exercised excessive action upon Israel issues in three things: 1) Israel is brought back to God; 2) the created things are restored; and 3) the all-inclusive Christ is ushered in. The restoration of the created yet fallen things goes along with Israel's return to God. God intends to restore the created and fallen things, but there is the need for Israel to usher in this restoration. When Israel turns to God, there will be the restoration of all things. Then the all-inclusive Christ will be ushered in. This is the divine philosophy in the book of Isaiah.

Especially in the first thirty-nine chapters of his prophecy, Isaiah's thought is focused on God's chastisement issuing in a return to God and bringing in the restoration and the all-inclusive Christ. This is the logic, the spiritual and heavenly philosophy, that dominates the book of Isaiah. Although this is not clearly written, it is nevertheless the basic and governing principle of Isaiah's writing. (*Life-study of Isaiah*, pp. 6-7, 111-112)

Further Reading: Life-study of Isaiah, msgs. 2-3, 17; *Gospel Outlines,* subj. 45

Enlightenment and inspiration: _____
_____
_____
_____

Morning Nourishment

Isa. The voice of one who cries in the wilderness: Make
40:3 clear the way of Jehovah; make straight in the desert
a highway for our God.
53:5 But He was wounded because of our transgressions; He was crushed because of our iniquities; the
chastening for our peace was upon Him, and by His
stripes we have been healed.
65:17 For I am now creating new heavens and a new earth,
and the former things will not be remembered, nor
will they come up in the heart.

It is not easy for us to know any book of the Bible. In the New
Testament, the most difficult book to enter into and to understand is Ephesians. In the Old Testament, the most difficult book
to enter into and to understand is Isaiah. As a book concerning
God's economy, Isaiah has its appearance, contents, and depths.
Furthermore, this book involves God's dealing with many nations
for a definite purpose.

The book of Isaiah, which has sixty-six chapters, is a representative of the Bible, which has sixty-six books. In these messages on
the book of Isaiah,…we will cover Isaiah in the way of a life-study,
not for knowledge or theology but for life.

To understand the book of Isaiah, we need to have the view
from the entire sixty-six books of the Bible. Isaiah is of two portions. The first portion includes chapters one through thirty-nine,
and the second portion includes chapters forty through sixty-six.
The first thirty-nine chapters of Isaiah correspond to the thirty-
nine books of the Old Testament. The last twenty-seven chapters
correspond to the twenty-seven books of the New Testament. The
New Testament begins with John the Baptist (Mark 1:1-3), and
Isaiah 40 also begins with John the Baptist (v. 3). (*Life-study of
Isaiah,* pp. 1-2, 119)

Today's Reading

The book of Isaiah speaks concerning salvation in such great
detail that some have even called it the Gospel of Isaiah. In it are

found prophecies concerning Christ: (a) His birth—God becoming a man (7:14; 9:6); (b) His genealogy—a descendant of Jesse (11:1); (c) His name—Immanuel, Wonderful Counselor, (a child being called) the Mighty God, (a son being called) the Eternal Father, the Prince of Peace, Jehovah's Servant (7:14; 9:6; 42:19); (d) His living—as a root out of a dry ground, having no form nor comeliness, His visage being marred more than any man, and His form more than the sons of men, being despised and forsaken of men, being a man of sorrows and acquainted with grief (52:14; 53:2-3); (e) His being anointed—being filled with the Spirit of God (61:1; 11:2); (f) His work—bringing good news and proclaiming God's jubilee (61:1-3); (g) His dealings with man—not crying out nor lifting up His voice, not breaking a bruised reed, and not quenching the smoking flax (42:1-4); (h) His death—having borne our sicknesses and carried our sorrows, being wounded for our transgressions and bruised for our iniquities (53:4a-10); (i) His burial—making His grave with the rich (53:9a); (j) His resurrection—swallowing up death, prolonging His days, justifying many (25:8a; 53:10b-11); (k) His coming back—rending the heavens and coming down, judging the people (64:1; 63:1-6); (l) His reign—in the millennium (Rev. 20:4, 6) reigning in righteousness, all peoples enjoying peace, and all creation living in harmony (Isa. 9:7; 11:3-16; 32:1; 33:17-24); (m) His kingdom—being exalted above all the nations and all peoples flowing to it (2:2-4; 35:1-10; Micah 4:1-3), bringing in the new heaven and new earth (Isa. 65:17; 66:22). Isaiah also prophesied that Christ, who became a man, was a sure foundation stone and a precious cornerstone laid by God for His building and trusted in by His believers (28:16), and that He would "be like a refuge from the wind / And a covering from the tempest, / Like streams of water in a dry place, / Like the shadow of a massive rock in a wasted land" (32:2). (*Truth Lessons—Level One,* vol. 2, pp. 29-30)

Further Reading: The Collected Works of Watchman Nee, vol. 17, pp. 111-120; *Life-study of Isaiah,* msg. 18

Enlightenment and inspiration: _____

_____

_____

_____

Morning Nourishment

Isa. In that day the Shoot of Jehovah will be beauty and
4:2 glory, and the fruit of the earth, excellence and splendor, to those of Israel who have escaped.
7:14 Therefore the Lord Himself will give you a sign:
Behold, the virgin will conceive and will bear a son,
and she will call his name Immanuel.
32:2 And a man will be like a refuge from the wind and a
covering from the tempest, like streams of water in
a dry place, like the shadow of a massive rock in a
wasted land.

According to Isaiah 4:2, the ushering in of Christ will be "in
that day," that is, in the day of the coming restoration of the nation
of Israel.

There are two striking expressions [in this verse]: *the Shoot of
Jehovah* and *the Fruit of the earth.* These two are one pair, illus-
trating Christ's two natures: the divine nature and the human
nature. The Shoot of Jehovah refers to Christ's deity, showing His
divine nature, and the Fruit of the earth (Luke 1:42) refers to
Christ's humanity with His human nature. As the Shoot of Jehovah, Christ comes out of God. As the Fruit of the earth, Christ,
having a human body made of dust, grows out of the earth. (*Life-
study of Isaiah,* p. 26)

Today's Reading

In the book of Isaiah, Christ is unveiled as the God-man, the
Shoot of Jehovah with beauty and glory and the Fruit of the earth
with excellence and splendor. In the restoration, to those of Israel
who have escaped, Christ in His deity will be beauty and glory,
and in His humanity He will be excellence and splendor.

The Shoot of Jehovah denotes that Christ is a new development of Jehovah God for the Triune God to branch out Himself in
His divinity into humanity. This is for Jehovah God's increase and
spread in the universe. The Fruit of the earth denotes that Christ,
as the divine Shoot of Jehovah, also becomes a man of flesh from
the earth. This is for the Triune God to be multiplied and

reproduced in humanity. As a man with the divine life, He is a seed, a grain of wheat, to produce many grains through His death and resurrection (John 12:24).

Such a God-man, Christ as the Shoot of Jehovah and the Fruit of the earth, is ushered in by God's judgment. In particular, He is ushered in by war, which is used by God to judge the nations. The more war there is, the more Christ will be ushered in. Many believers can testify that they were saved during a time of war.

Out of the Christ who is ushered in by judgment issues the restoration of the nation of Israel. Therefore, God's judgment eventually results in Christ, the God-man, with restoration.

Isaiah 32:2 says, "A man will be like a refuge from the wind / And a covering from the tempest, / Like streams of water in a dry place, / Like the shadow of a massive rock in a wasted land." Here we see that Christ will also be a man who is a refuge from the wind, a covering from the tempest, like streams of water in a dry place, and like the shadow of a massive rock in a wasted land. On the one hand, Christ will be the King ruling; on the other hand, He will be a man overshadowing. Under Him there will be righteousness, protection, and enjoyment. This is a picture of the millennial kingdom. (*Life-study of Isaiah,* pp. 26-27, 122)

The child born of a human virgin (Isa. 7:14) is the Son given by the Eternal Father. Christ is the child born of both the divine and human natures (Matt. 1:20-23), and He is also the Son in the divine nature given by the Eternal Father. Through the birth of the divine-human child, the Eternal Father gave us His divine Son as a gift. Through such a giving, everyone who believes in, that is, receives, this dear Son receives eternal life (John 3:16; 1 John 5:11-12). (Isa. 9:6, footnote 1)

As the child born to us, Christ is the Mighty God (Matt. 2:11; Rom. 9:5; Heb. 1:8), and as the Son given to us, He is the Eternal Father (Isa. 63:16; 64:8; John 5:43; 10:30; 14:7-10). (footnote 5)

Further Reading: Life-study of Isaiah, msg. 4

Enlightenment and inspiration: _____

_____

_____

_____

Morning Nourishment

Isa. All the flocks of Kedar will be gathered together
60:7 to you; the rams of Nebaioth will minister to you;
they will go up acceptably upon My altar, and I will
beautify the house of My beauty.

13 The glory of Lebanon will come to you, the fir tree,
the pine tree, and the box tree together, to beautify the place of My sanctuary; and I will make the
place for My feet glorious.

In the New Jerusalem (Rev. 21:23) Israel will enjoy Jehovah in Christ, the Servant of Jehovah, as the eternal light (Isa.
60:19-22). Verses 19 through 21 say, "You will no longer have the
sun for your light by day, / Nor for brightness will the moon give
you light; / But Jehovah will be an eternal light to you, / And your
God your beauty. / Your sun will no longer go down, / Nor will
your moon withdraw; / For Jehovah will be an eternal light to
you, / And the days of your mourning will be ended. / Then all
your people will be righteous; / They will possess the land forever, / The branch of My planting, / The works of My hands, /
That I may be beautified." Israel will have something brighter
than the sun and the moon, for they will have Jehovah as an
eternal light to them.

Verse 21 says that God will be beautified in Israel. Many
translations say *glorified,* but *beautified* is a more accurate rend-
ering of the Hebrew word. Restored Israel will be God's beautification. In the restoration Israel will be glorified and beautified
and thus become God's beautification. God will be beautified by
the restored and beautified Israel. (*Life-study of Isaiah,* p. 210)

Today's Reading

In Isaiah chapters fifty-nine and sixty, Christ is unveiled as
our Redeemer. Having passed through incarnation, human living, crucifixion, and resurrection, He is now the saving One, saving His people from their sins and iniquities and becoming their
light and glory. By putting Himself into us as the Spirit and the
word, He becomes our beauty, brightness, and splendor. By

means of the life-giving Spirit and the word, which is the embodiment of Christ, we receive the divine dispensing. The more He dispenses Himself into us as life and everything to us, the more we become bright, beautiful, and glorious. This is Christ becoming our light and glory. Eventually, we will become God's glory and beauty. He becomes our beauty so that we may become His beauty. In this way God and His chosen people are glorified and beautified in mutuality.

The Shoot of Jehovah is a new development of Jehovah God for His increase and spreading through His incarnation (Isa. 7:14; Matt. 1:22-23)....Christ as the Shoot of Jehovah is for the branching out of Jehovah God, in His divinity, into humanity (John 1:14).

The incarnated God, in His divinity, will be the beauty and glory of God's chosen people in the day of restoration. Because Christ lives in us, we are partakers of the divine nature (2 Pet. 1:4). In this sense, we are not only human but also divine. The divine nature is our beauty and our glory. When worldly women go to a special place, they may adorn themselves with the best material and jewelry. This is for their beauty and glory. The uniform of generals in an army is full of stars and badges. This is also for their beauty and glory. Our beauty and glory is not in such outward adornment. Our God with His divine nature is our beauty and our glory. In the day of restoration, if we are faithful, we will be the most beautiful and glorious creatures in this universe because we will have our God in a full way as our beauty and as our glory. Even today if we live Christ, those around us will see that we are weighty and dignified. When a man lives Christ, people will consider that he is a weighty man, a man of gravity, a man of beauty and glory beyond description. Whatever we do and say in Christ is full of dignity and gravity. We should not forget our divine genealogy. We are sons of God in the family of God. His divinity is our beauty and our glory. (*Life-study of Isaiah,* pp. 210, 224-226)

Further Reading: Life-study of Isaiah, msgs. 30, 33

Enlightenment and inspiration: _____
_____
_____
_____

[handwritten marginalia: "Lord Jesus save me from this deception"]
[handwritten marginalia: "Luke 18 v30"]
[handwritten marginalia top right: "Lord I don't want to be a part of 'This people'"]

Morning Nourishment

Isa.
29:13   And the Lord said, Because this people draws near
with their mouth, and with their lips they honor Me,
yet they remove their heart far from Me, and their fear
for Me is a commandment of men *merely* learned.

40:31   …Those who wait on Jehovah will renew *their*
strength; they will mount up with wings like eagles;
they will run and will not faint; they will walk and
will not become weary.

62:6-7   Upon your walls, O Jerusalem, I have appointed
watchmen; all day and all night they will never keep
silent. You who remind Jehovah, do not be dumb; and
do not give Him quiet until He establishes and until
He makes Jerusalem a praise in the earth.

[handwritten marginalia: "This includes Me."]

If we are clean, clear, and full of understanding, we will realize
that the situation among humankind today is of two aspects.
First, everyone is drunk. People are drunk with today's modern
fashion and style. They do not love the Lord but love other things.
Second, people are not genuine, not true, but false. This is the situation of fallen humankind. Even among God's elect drunken-
ness and hypocrisy may be present. If we do not pray with a
watchful spirit, these two things may enter into the church life.
God's people may become drunken by loving things other than
the Lord, and they may be hypocritical in their praying and testi-
fying. Whenever this kind of situation invades God's elect, He
must come in to exercise His judgment upon the drunkards and
upon hypocrisy in worship. (*Life-study of Isaiah,* p. 110)

[handwritten marginalia: "This is the only way"]

Today's Reading

The northern kingdom of Israel was full of drunkards (Isa. 28),
and the southern kingdom of Judah was full of hypocritical worshippers. These two conditions characterize the condition of
fallen mankind on the earth. First, people are drunk by loving
things other than the Lord, and second, they are not true but
false. The kind of hypocritical worship described in this verse con-
tinued until the time of Christ (Matt. 15:1-14; John 4:20-24). As

revealed in Isaiah 29:1-12, 14-16, Jehovah judged the hypocrisy of the worshippers in Jerusalem. (Isa. 29:13, footnote 1)

With the hypocritical worship spoken of in Isaiah 29, there was vanity but no reality (v. 13) and blindness but no wisdom (vv. 9-12, 15-16). Through His incarnation Christ brought to us the very reality of the universe—the Triune God, the Divine Trinity, embodied in a person, Jesus Christ (John 1:14, 17). When we realize the embodied reality, the Divine Trinity in Christ, our eyes, our ears, and our understanding are opened, and we have wisdom. Christ is the reality and wisdom to God's redeemed people (John 14:6a; 1 Cor. 1:24, 30) that makes them true worshippers of God (John 4:23-24). (Isa. 29:15, footnote 1)

To wait on the eternal God (Isa. 40:28) means that we terminate ourselves, that is, that we stop ourselves with our living, our doing, and our activity, and receive God in Christ as our life, our person, and our replacement. Such a waiting one will be renewed and strengthened to such an extent that he will mount up with wings like eagles. He will not only walk and run but also soar in the heavens, far above every earthly frustration. This is a transformed person. Isaiah 40 leads us to a comparison between Hezekiah, a godly man who was still in the old creation (chs. 36—39), and a regenerated and transformed person in the new creation.

In Isaiah 40 there are the announcing of the gospel (corresponding to the four Gospels—vv. 1-5), salvation through regeneration (corresponding to the Acts—Isa. 40:6-8), and transformation (corresponding to the Epistles—vv. 28-31). (Isa. 40:31, footnote 1)

The eagles' wings signify the resurrection power of Christ, God's power in life, becoming our grace (cf. 1 Cor. 15:10; 2 Cor. 4:7; 12:9a). Those who stop themselves and wait on Jehovah will experience the power of resurrection, will be transformed, and will soar in the heavens (cf. Phil. 4:13; Col. 1:11). (footnote 2)

Further Reading: Life-study of Isaiah, msgs. 16, 21, 44

Enlightenment and inspiration: _____

_____

_____

_____

Hymns, #541

1 Not the law of letters,
   But the Christ of life
   God desires to give us,
   Saving us from strife;
   It is not some doctrine,
   But 'tis Christ Himself
   Who alone releases
   From our sinful self.

2 Any kind of teaching,
   Any kind of form,
   Cannot quicken spirits
   Or our souls transform;
   It is Christ as Spirit
   Gives us life divine,
   Thus thru us to live the
   Life of God's design.

3 Not philosophy nor
   Any element
   Can to Christ conform us
   As His complement;
   But 'tis Christ Himself who
   All our nature takes
   And in resurrection
   Us His members makes.

4 Not religion, even
   Christianity,
   Can fulfill God's purpose
   Or economy;
   But 'tis Christ within us
   As our all in all
   Satisfies God's wishes,
   And His plan withal.

5 All the gifts we're given
   By the Lord in grace,
   All the different functions
   Cannot Christ replace.
   Only Christ Himself must
   Be our all in all!
   Only Christ Himself in
   All things, great or small!

Composition for prophecy with main point and sub-points: _____

_____

_____

_____

_____

_____

_____

_____

_____

_____

_____

_____

_____

_____

_____

_____

_____

_____

_____

_____

_____

_____

_____

_____

_____

_____

_____

_____

_____

_____

_____

_____

_____

_____

_____

_____

_____

_____

The Revelation of the Lord Jehovah, the Eternal God

Scripture Reading: Isa. 1:2, 4; 25:8; 40:28; 45:15; 29:16; 54:5; 12:2-3; 66:2

Day 1   I. **Elohim is the name of God in relation to creation, whereas Jehovah is the name of God in relation to man (Gen. 1:1; 2:4; Isa. 1:2, 4):**

Very mysterious A. *Jehovah* means "I am who I am," indicating that Jehovah is the self-existing and ever-existing eternal One, the One who was in the past, who is in the present, and who will be in the future forever (Exo. 3:14; Rev. 1:4):

1. Jehovah is the only One who is and who depends on nothing apart from Himself, and we must believe that He is (Heb. 11:6).
2. As the I Am, He is the all-inclusive One, the reality of every positive thing and of whatever His people need (John 6:35; 8:12; 10:14; 11:25; 14:6).

B. Jehovah in the Old Testament is the Jesus in the New Testament (Matt. 1:21):

1. *Jesus* means "Jehovah the Savior," or "the salvation of Jehovah"; hence, Jesus is not only a man but Jehovah, and not only Jehovah but Jehovah becoming our salvation (v. 21).
2. As the great I Am, the Lord Jesus is the eternal, ever-existing God who has a relationship with man; anyone who does not believe that Jesus is I Am will die in his sins (John 8:24, 28, 58).

C. The Lord Jehovah is the Lord Jesus Christ; the Lord Jehovah is the Old Testament Lord Jesus Christ, and the Lord Jesus Christ is the New Testament Lord Jehovah (Isa. 25:8; Eph. 1:2).

II. **The Lord Jehovah is the eternal God (Isa. 40:28):**

A. In Hebrew *the eternal God* is *Elohey Olam* (cf. *El Olam*, Gen. 21:33):

1. *El,* meaning "the Mighty One," is one of the

Judgment the formation of an oppinion after deliberation= concederation. An oppinon so pronounced

23 WEEK 2 — OUTLINE

It's working out is it's chastening bad situations names of God; *Olam,* meaning "eternal" or "eternity," comes from a Hebrew root meaning "to conceal, to hide."

2. The full meaning of this title indicates that the Lord Jehovah is the mysterious Mighty One in eternity.

Day 2 B. The divine title *El Olam* implies eternal life (John 1:4; 3:15); by calling on the name of Jehovah, the Eternal Mighty One, Abraham experienced God as the ever-living, secret, mysterious One, who is the eternal life (Gen. 21:33; John 20:31).

III. **The Lord Jehovah is <u>the only God</u> (Isa. 40:18; 44:6, 8, 24):**

A. Jehovah is the unique Creator—the majestic, exalted One, who inhabits eternity (Gen. 1:1; Rev. 4:11; Isa. 42:5; 45:18; 57:15; 2:10-21; 10:34).

B. As the holy and righteous One, Jehovah deals with people according to what He is (51:8; 17:7; 29:23; 24:16):

1. Righteousness is the base for holiness, and on this base holiness is exhibited; with His righteousness as the base, God shows Himself as the holy God, in righteousness exhibiting His holiness (5:16).

2. God's chastening and disciplining is to uplift us from righteousness to holiness (Heb. 12:5-11):

a. In His salvation He first justifies us to make us righteous in Christ, and then He sanctifies us to make us holy (Rom. 3:24; 6:19, 22).

b. To be righteous is to match God's way of doing things outwardly, but to be holy is to match God's <u>nature inwardly</u>; hence, holiness is higher than righteousness (Phil. 3:9; Heb. 12:10, 14; Rev. 19:8; 21:2; 22:11).

c. While the Lord is chastening us, we should wait for Him in the path of His judging in order to learn the lesson that He would give us; God's judgments always teach us lessons in righteousness (Isa. 26:8-9).

IV. **The Lord Jehovah is triune (6:8; 11:2; 42:1; 61:1; Matt. 28:19; 2 Cor. 13:14):**

  A. The Lord Jehovah—the threefold yet one unique God—is the God of Abraham, the God of Isaac, and the God of Jacob; this implies that He is the Triune God—the Father, the Son, and the Spirit (Exo. 3:6, 14-15; Matt. 28:19).

  B. The words *I* and *Us* in Isaiah 6:8 indicate that the One speaking here is triune, that He is not merely Christ but Christ as the embodiment of the Triune God (Col. 2:9; John 1:1, 14; 12:41).

  C. According to the entire divine revelation in the Scriptures, the Triune God is for God's dispensing: the Father as the origin is the fountain, the Son as the expression is the spring, and the Spirit as the transmission is the flow (John 4:14; 7:37-39; Rev. 22:1-2; Isa. 12:2-3).

Day 3 V. **The Lord Jehovah is a God who hides Himself (45:15):**

  A. Although our God is omnipresent, omnipotent, and full of forgiveness, He is also the hiding God, as the book of Esther indicates; He created the universe and then hid Himself within it, until we do not know where to find Him (Job 23:3-9).

  B. We need to realize that the omnipotent God whom we are serving is still hiding Himself, especially when He is helping us (John 14:26; Rom. 8:26):

   1. We cannot see Him, and apparently He is not doing anything; actually, in a hidden way He is doing many things for us (vv. 28, 34; Esth. 4:14).

   2. Silently, secretly, and ceaselessly, the God who hides Himself is working within us (Phil. 2:13).

VI. **The Lord Jehovah reveals Himself by speaking (Isa. 40:5, 8):**

  A. Without His speaking, God is mysterious, but He has revealed Himself in His speaking, and now He is the revealed God (Heb. 1:1; Isa. 40:5, 8).

  B. Jesus was sent by God for the purpose of speaking

the word of God for God's expression (John 3:34a; 7:16; 14:24):

1. The word of God is actually Christ, the embodiment of God (Isa. 40:8; Col. 2:9).
2. In the word—the speaking—of Jesus, God is unveiled and presented to men so that they may see God (John 14:7-10).
3. The Son, as the Word of God and the speaking of God, has declared God with a full expression, explanation, and definition of Him (1:1, 14, 18).

Day 4 **VII. The Lord Jehovah is the Potter (Isa. 29:16; 64:8; Jer. 18:6; Rom. 9:20-21):**

A. Jehovah is the Potter, and we are the clay in His hand (Jer. 18:1-6).
B. As the Potter, God is sovereign and has absolute authority over us; He has the right to do whatever He desires (Rom. 9:20-21):
   1. If He wills, He can make one vessel unto honor and another unto dishonor; this does not depend on our choice—it depends on God's sovereignty (v. 21).
   2. It is of God's sovereignty that He, the Potter, makes the riches of His glory known by creating vessels of mercy to contain Himself (v. 23).

VIII. The Lord Jehovah is our Husband (Isa. 54:5):

A. The entire Bible is a divine romance, a record of how God courts His chosen people and eventually marries them (Gen. 2:21-24; Rev. 19:7; 21:2, 9-10).
B. Both the Major Prophets and the Minor Prophets speak of God as the Husband and of God's chosen people as the wife (Isa. 62:5; Hosea 2:16, 19).
C. The crucial emphasis of the revelation released by all the prophets from Isaiah to Malachi is that God wants to have an organic union with His chosen people (Isa. 62:5; Jer. 2:2; 3:14; 31:32; Ezek. 16:8; 23:5; Hosea 2:7, 19):
   1. In this union God is His people's life, and they are His expression.

     2. In this way God and His chosen people become a universal couple; this is God's intention in His eternal economy (John 3:29; 2 Cor. 11:2; Rev. 22:17).

Day 5 **IX. The Lord Jehovah is our salvation (Isa. 12:2-3; 17:10; 1:18):**

A. Isaiah 12:2 clearly reveals that salvation is God Himself; in the New Testament Jah Jehovah, who is salvation, is Jesus, the incarnated God (Luke 2:30).

B. As the eternal Rock, Christ is the God of our salvation (Isa. 17:10).

C. In God's full salvation He not only forgives our sins, exempting us from the penalty of our sins and removing the record of our sins from before Him; He also washes away the traces of sins in us, making us as white as snow and white like wool (1:18):

    1. The washing that makes us as white as snow is a positional washing from without through the blood of Jesus Christ (1 John 1:7; Heb. 1:3b; Rev. 1:5).

    2. The washing that makes us white like wool is a washing of our nature metabolically from within by God's Spirit and by His life (1 Cor. 6:11; Titus 3:5).

X. The Lord Jehovah has become the divine water (Isa. 12:3; 55:1):

A. Both the Old Testament and the New Testament show that God's practical salvation is the processed Triune God Himself as the living water (12:2-3; 55:1; Rev. 7:10, 14, 17; 21:6; 22:1, 17).

B. In the book of Isaiah God considers that He is our salvation as living water (12:2-3; 55:1):

    1. To be our salvation, the Triune God was processed to become the life-giving Spirit as the living water, the water of life (1 Cor. 15:45b; John 7:37-39).

    2. The waters in Isaiah 55:1 and Revelation 22:17 are the redeeming God, the very God who accomplished redemption for us through His

incarnation, human living, crucifixion, and resurrection.

3. In totality, what Christ is and has accomplished is just the divine water, which is the consummated Spirit as the consummation of the Triune God for us to drink and enjoy (Isa. 55:1; John 7:37-39; 1 Cor. 12:13).

Day 6   **XI. The Lord Jehovah will deal with His enemies (Isa. 14:12-15; 24:21; 27:1):**

A. Isaiah identifies Lucifer with Nebuchadnezzar, the king of Babylon, thus regarding him as a figure of Satan, as one who was one with Satan; this unveils Satan's kingdom of darkness behind the nations and his oneness with the rulers of the nations (14:4, 12-15; Ezek. 28:12; Dan. 10:13, 20; Eph. 6:12b).

B. In Isaiah 24:21 *the host on high* refers to Satan and his angels in the air (cf. Eph. 2:2; 6:12); Jehovah's reaction to the nations' excessive action on Israel deals both with Satan's army in the air and with the kings on the earth (Rev. 12:7-10; 11:15).

XII. The Lord Jehovah desires to have as His dwelling place a group of people into whom He can enter (Isa. 57:15; 66:2):

A. God intends to have a dwelling place in the universe that is the mingling of God and man, in which God is built into man and man is built into God, so that God and man, man and God, can be a mutual abode to each other (John 14:2, 20, 23; 15:4; 1 John 4:13).

B. In the New Testament this dwelling place, this house, is the church, which is God's habitation in the believers' spirit (Eph. 2:22; 1 Tim. 3:15).

C. The ultimate manifestation of this universal building, this universal house, is the New Jerusalem; in this city God is in man, taking man as His dwelling place, and man is in God, taking God as his habitation (Rev. 21:3, 22; Gen. 28:12, 17; 2 Sam. 7:12-14).

Morning Nourishment

Exo. **And God said to Moses, I AM WHO I AM. And He said,**
3:14 **Thus you shall say to the children of Israel, I AM has**
sent me to you.
John **Jesus said to them, Truly, truly, I say to you, Before**
8:58 **Abraham came into being, I am.**

Jehovah means I Am Who I Am, the self-existing and ever-existing One. Exodus 3:13-14 says, "Then Moses said to God, If I come to the children of Israel and say to them, The God of your fathers has sent me to you, and they say to me, What is His name? what shall I say to them? And God said to Moses, I AM WHO I AM. And He said, Thus you shall say to the children of Israel, I AM has sent me to you." God called Moses and charged him to say to Israel that His name is I Am. *Jehovah* means I Am, I Am Who I Am.

We can also say that *Jehovah* means I was, I am, and I will be. Revelation 1:4 refers to God as the One "who is and who was and who is coming." He is the One who was in the past, who is in the present, and who will be in the future. In other words, He is self-existing and ever-existing, implying that He has no beginning and no ending. (*The History of God in His Union with Man,* pp. 10-11)

Today's Reading

His being the I Am means "I am whatever you need" and "I am everything." We have a signed check with the space for the amount left blank, and we may fill in whatever we need. After the name "I Am" we can fill in the amount. The heavenly bank will cash this check. The Lord is whatever we need. If we need salvation, light, life, power, wisdom, holiness, or righteousness, Jesus Christ Himself is all these things to us. He is Jehovah God, the great I Am.

Another name for God is the Hebrew title *Elohim,* implying the faithful strong One (Gen. 1:1; 2:4). The word *Elohim* is plural in number. This indicates that God is triune. Genesis 1:1 says that in the beginning God (Elohim) created the heaven and the earth. (*The History of God in His Union with Man,* p. 11)

As the self-existing One and ever-existing One, God is the reality of every positive thing. The Gospel of John reveals that He is all we need: life, light, food, drink, the pasture, the way, and everything. Therefore, this title of God indicates not only that He exists eternally but also that, in a positive sense, He is everything. Do you need life? God is life. Do you want light? God is light. Do you desire holiness? God is holiness. God exists from eternity to eternity, and He is everything. This is our God. (*The Conclusion of the New Testament,* p. 54)

The Lord Jesus told the Pharisees, "Unless you believe that I am, you will die in your sins" (John 8:24b). Eventually, they asked Him, "You are not yet fifty years old, and have You seen Abraham?" Jesus responded, "Truly, truly, I say to you, Before Abraham came into being, I am" (vv. 57-58). The Lord as the great I Am is the eternal, ever-existing God. Hence, He was before Abraham and is greater than Abraham (v. 53). The name *Jesus* means "Jehovah the Savior." Jesus is Jehovah, the eternal I Am. (*The Crucial Points of the Major Items of the Lord's Recovery Today,* p. 6)

The last twenty-seven chapters of Isaiah are the second section of this book, and they correspond to the twenty-seven books of the New Testament. This section of twenty-seven chapters can be considered as the essence of the New Testament, the extract of the real significance of the New Testament. This extract is concerning one person. Today we call Him the Lord Jesus Christ, which equals the Lord Jehovah in the Old Testament. The Lord Jehovah is the Old Testament Lord Jesus Christ, and the Lord Jesus Christ is the New Testament Lord Jehovah.

Isaiah 40 presents a marvelous picture of the all-inclusive Christ as Jehovah the Savior. Through His living and abiding word, we have been regenerated. We have been fed by Him to know Him as the Holy One, the eternal God, Jehovah, the Creator of the heavens and the earth. He is unlimited, unsearchable, incomparable, and high. (*Life-study of Isaiah,* pp. 317-318, 316)

Further Reading: The Collected Works of Watchman Nee, vol. 9, pp. 263-274; *The Central Line of the Divine Revelation,* msg. 1; *The Conclusion of the New Testament,* msg. 26

Enlightenment and inspiration: _____

_____
_____
_____

Morning Nourishment

Isa. But Jehovah of hosts is exalted in judgment, and the
5:16 holy God shows Himself holy in righteousness.
26:8 Indeed in the path of Your judgments, O Jehovah, we
have waited for You. Your name, that is, Your memorial, is the desire of *our* soul.

Eternal life is a divine person who is so concealed, veiled, hidden,
mysterious, secret, and yet so real, ever-existing, and ever-living,
without beginning or ending. The title *El Olam* [Gen. 21:33, footnote 3] implies eternal life. Here God was not revealed to Abraham
but was experienced by him as the ever-living, secret, mysterious
One who is the eternal life....Abraham experienced God as the eternal life...[and] could testify to the whole universe that he was experiencing the hidden, ever-living One as his mysterious life. There,
at Beer-sheba, he called on the name of Jehovah, El Olam....After
having so much experience, with Isaac at Beer-sheba under the
tamarisk tree he experienced the ever-living, mysterious One as
his inner life and called, "O Jehovah, El Olam!" Although no one
could see this mysterious One, He was real to Abraham in his experience. The One we have within us today is the very El Olam, the
hidden, secret, concealed, mysterious, ever-living One. He is our
life. We may have the same enjoyment Abraham had simply by
calling, "O Lord Jesus." (*Life-study of Genesis*, p. 749)

Today's Reading

In His judgment over the nations, Jehovah of hosts is exalted,
and the holy God shows Himself holy in righteousness (Isa. 5:16).
If we are not righteous, we cannot be holy. Without righteousness
there is no base for being holy. Righteousness is the base for holiness,
and upon this base holiness is exhibited. Hence, holiness is higher
than righteousness. With His righteousness as the base, God shows
Himself as the holy God. In righteousness He exhibits His holiness.

God could expect only righteousness from the nations because
they are not the sons of God. It is with His sons that God expects
to see holiness (Heb. 12:5-11). God's chastening and disciplining are to
uplift us from righteousness to holiness. In His salvation, He first

justified us to make us righteous in Christ. After this, we need to go on to be sanctified, to be made holy. To be righteous is to match God's way of doing things outwardly, but to be holy is to match God's nature inwardly. As the sons of God, we need to go on from righteousness to reach holiness, to show ourselves holy in righteousness.

While the Lord is chastening us, we need to learn something of Him and find out the lesson that the Lord would give us. However, some saints, after being chastened by the Lord, seem to learn nothing. They waste both their time and the Lord's chastening. Whenever we are chastened by the Lord, we need to learn something of Him. This is to wait for Him in the path of His judgments [Isa. 26:8]....God's judgment always teaches us lessons in righteousness. (*Life-study of Isaiah,* pp. 17-18, 98-99)

As the I Am, He is the God of Abraham, the God of Isaac, and the God of Jacob (Exo. 3:15). In His person there is the Father like Abraham, the Son like Isaac, and the Spirit like Jacob. As Jehovah, He is the threefold yet one unique God.

According to the entire revelation...of the Bible, the Divine Trinity—the Father, the Son, and the Spirit—is for God's dispensing, that is, for the distribution of God into His chosen people. God's desire with His strong intention is to dispense Himself into His chosen people as their life, as their life supply, and as their everything. To carry out this dispensing He needs to be triune.

The Father as the origin is the fountain; the Son as the expression is the spring; and the Spirit as the transmission is the flow. The Spirit as the flow is the reaching, the application, of the Triune God for the distribution of Himself into His chosen people. A fountain is the origin, the source, of a stream, or river; a spring is the emergence, the expression, of the fountain; and the stream or river is the flow [Jer. 2:13; John 4:14; Rev. 22:1]. (*The Crucial Points of the Major Items of the Lord's Recovery Today,* p. 7)

Further Reading: The Crucial Points of the Major Items of the Lord's Recovery Today, pp. 5-15; The Conclusion of the New Testament, msg. 5; The Collected Works of Witness Lee, 1965, vol. 4, pp. 545-547

Enlightenment and inspiration: _____

_____

_____

_____

Morning Nourishment

Isa. **Surely You are a God who hides Himself, O God of**
45:15 **Israel, the Savior.**

40:5 **Then the glory of Jehovah will be revealed, and all**
flesh will see *it* together, because the mouth of Jeho-
vah has spoken.

Judging & mding
Judsinge
midding

In His secret care the hiding God raised up Esther, a Jewish orphan virgin, to be crowned by the top king as his queen....Esther saved the king from being assassinated, telling the king in Morde-cai's name of those who planned to assassinate him [Esther 2:1-23].

Our God is omnipresent, omnipotent, merciful, and full of for-giveness. Although He is such a God, He is also the hiding God. Because our God is a hiding God, others may check with us and ask, "Where is your God? Where is His kingdom?" When we are questioned in such a manner, we may want to answer in this way: "My God is hidden. I cannot see Him, and you cannot see Him either. But you need to realize that sooner or later my hidden God will come in to do something on my behalf and to deal with those who do not believe in Him."

Today we need to realize that the omnipotent God whom we are serving is still hiding Himself, especially when He is helping us. We cannot see Him, and apparently He is not doing anything for us. Actually, He is with us all the time and, in a hidden way, He is doing many things for us. (*Life-study of Esther,* pp. 3-5)

Today's Reading

The God who hides Himself is at work within your life, and He is working mightily. Your responsibility is to cooperate with Him by responding to His voice within—that "still small voice," that voice that seems so much a part of your own feelings that you scarcely recognize it as a voice at all. To that voice, registered in the deepest depths of your being, you must say, "Amen," for there, secretly and ceaselessly, the God who hides Himself is working. (Watchman Nee, *A God Who Hides Himself,* p. 20)

Isaiah 40:5 also indicates that Jehovah is revealed through His speaking (John 3:34a; 7:17). In the Gospel of John, the Lord

Jesus told us that He was sent by the Father (5:36b-37a) and that He did not speak from Himself (14:10). He was speaking from His Father, His teaching was altogether of His Father, and His speaking was the expression of the Father. The more you listen to His speaking, the more you see Jehovah. John 3:34a says, "For He whom God has sent speaks the words of God." He was sent by God for the purpose of speaking the word of God for God's expression. In other words, His speaking was the revealing of God. When you listen to Him, you see God. In His word, His speaking, God is unveiled and presented to you.

Jesus is still speaking, and His words remain forever. When we hear His word, we see Him. We were saved by hearing His word. Some may say that at a certain time they saw Jesus and were saved. Actually, they did not see Him physically, but they heard His word. His word is just Himself, and He is Jehovah, and Jehovah is God. Thus, we may say that the word is God. In the beginning was the Word, and the Word was God (John 1:1). When I speak, I always exercise not to speak from myself. I exercise to speak the word of the Lord. When we speak in this way, the Lord is present in our speaking, and others are able to see Jesus. When we are under the ministry of the Lord's word, we see Jesus, Jehovah, the Savior, God, the glad tidings. All of these are one. This is why we, the saved ones, like to come to the meetings. In the meetings there is the speaking of the Lord, the word of God. When we hear His word, we see Him. (*Life-study of Isaiah,* p. 312)

As the One in whom the fullness of the Godhead dwells bodily, Christ is the embodiment of the Triune God. The Son is God Himself expressed (Heb. 1:8). God the Father is hidden; God the Son is expressed. No one has ever seen God; the Son, as the Word of God (John 1:1; Rev. 19:13) and the speaking of God (Heb. 1:1-2), has declared Him in a full expression, explanation, and definition (John 1:18). (*The Conclusion of the New Testament,* pp. 2768-2769)

Further Reading: A God Who Hides Himself; Life-study of Esther, msg. 1; *Life-study of Isaiah,* msg. 44

Enlightenment and inspiration: _____

_____
_____
_____

Morning Nourishment

Isa. **But now, Jehovah, You are our Father; we are the**
64:8 **clay; and You, our Potter; and all of us are the work**
of Your hand.

54:5 **For your Maker is your Husband; Jehovah of hosts**
is His name. And the Holy One of Israel is your
Redeemer; He is called the God of all the earth.

Jeremiah 18:1-10 reveals Jehovah as the sovereign Potter, the One with the absolute right over His pottery....Jehovah told Jeremiah to go down to the potter's house (vv. 1-2). Jeremiah saw that the potter was working and reworking the pottery at his wheel into another vessel, as it seemed good for him to make (vv. 3-4). This indicates that the potter has the full right to do whatever he desires with the clay.

Jehovah as the sovereign Potter is able to do with the house of Israel, as the clay in His hand, in changeable ways according to Israel's condition (vv. 6-10). Verse 6 says, "Am I not able to do with you, O house of Israel, as this potter does? declares Jehovah. Indeed, as the clay is in the hand of the potter, so you are in My hand, O house of Israel." (*Life-study of Jeremiah*, p. 122)

Today's Reading

Although the words *sovereign* or *sovereignty* are not used in Romans 9:20 and 21, these verses certainly refer to God's sovereignty: "But rather, O man, who are you who answer back to God? Shall the thing molded say to him who molded it, Why did you make me thus? Or does not the potter have authority over the clay to make out of the same lump one vessel unto honor and another unto dishonor?" We all need to realize who we are. We are God's creatures, and He is our Creator. As His creatures, we should not resist His purpose (v. 19) or answer back to Him, the Creator....God is the Potter, and we are the clay. As the Potter, God is sovereign. He has authority over the clay. If He wills, He can make one vessel to honor and another to dishonor. This does not depend on our choice—it depends on God's sovereignty.

God has the authority to make the ones He has selected and

called, not only from among the Jews but also from among the Gentiles, vessels of mercy to contain Him in order that His glory might be manifested. (*The Conclusion of the New Testament*, pp. 113-114)

The entire Bible is a book of engagement. In the Scriptures we have a record of how God courts His chosen people and eventually marries them. For eternity, the Triune God as the Husband will enjoy a sweet married life with His wife, His chosen and redeemed people. The New Jerusalem will even be called the wife of the Lamb (Rev. 21:9). The conclusion of the Bible is the marriage of God and His people. Since the Bible ends in this way, it can truly be called a book of engagement. The main subject of the Scriptures is God's engagement to His people. If this were not the main subject of the Bible, the Bible would not conclude with a word concerning the universal marriage of God and His redeemed ones. (*Life-study of Exodus*, pp. 636-637)

The crucial emphasis of the revelation released by all the prophets from Isaiah to Malachi is that God wants to have an organic union with His chosen people, like the union of Adam with Eve. In the writings of the prophets, God expresses His desire to have an organic union with His chosen people, making Himself their life and making them His expression. In this way God and His chosen people become a couple, a compound person, just as Adam and Eve became a couple. Originally Adam was alone, but later Eve came out of Adam. Eve was built from Adam's rib to match Adam, to marry Adam, and to be Adam's counterpart (Gen. 2:21-22). Eventually, the two became one in nature and in life. This is a type of what God desires. God's desire is to be united with His chosen people to be a universal couple, which in Revelation 22:17 is called "the Spirit and the bride." Because this is God's intention in His eternal economy, both the Major Prophets and the Minor Prophets speak of God as the Husband and of God's chosen people as the wife. (*Life-study of the Minor Prophets*, pp. 9-10)

Further Reading: Life-study of Jeremiah, msg. 18; Life-study of Exodus, msg. 54; Life-study of the Minor Prophets, msg. 1

Enlightenment and inspiration: _____

_____

_____

_____

Morning Nourishment

Isa. **God is now my salvation; I will trust and not dread;**
12:2-3 **for Jah Jehovah is my strength and song, and He**
has become my salvation. Therefore you will draw
water with rejoicing from the springs of salvation.

Isaiah 12:2 clearly reveals that salvation is God Himself. In
the New Testament Jah Jehovah, who is salvation, is Jesus, the
incarnated God (Matt. 1:21 and footnote; Luke 2:30 and footnote).
(Isa. 12:2, footnote 1)

In this verse strength and song both indicate experience. When
God's salvation is experienced by us, it becomes our strength, and
eventually it will be our song, our praising. (footnote 3)

Today's Reading

Every human being apart from Christ has nothing to trust in,
but we have the Lord as the eternal Rock to trust in. Isaiah 17:10
says, "For you have forgotten the God of your salvation, / And the
Rock of your stronghold you have not remembered. / Therefore
you plant plants of delight / And set them with plant cuttings to a
strange god." Christ is the God of our salvation. Actually, He Himself is our salvation. He is the Rock of stronghold for His people to
remember Him as their salvation....We have to pray, "Lord, we do
not ever want to plant plants for another god. We want to always
remember You." As the Rock of our stronghold, Christ is the God
of our salvation in whom we should trust.

He is also the Rock of Israel for His people to contact Him as
their joy. Isaiah 30:29 says, "You will have a song / As in the night
when the feast is sanctified, / And gladness of heart as when one
marches to the flute / To go to the mountain of Jehovah, to the
Rock of Israel." Although this verse describes the coming age of
restoration, we enjoy a foretaste of this in the meetings of the
church and the ministry. (*Life-study of Isaiah,* p. 285)

In God's full salvation He not only forgives our sins, exempting
us from the penalty of our sins and removing the record of our sins
from before Him; He also washes away the traces of sins in us,
making us as white as snow and white like wool [Isa. 1:18]. Both

snow and wool are naturally white. Hence, as a result of God's washing, we become not only white but also naturally white, as if we had never been defiled. The washing that makes us as white as snow is a positional washing from without through the blood of Jesus Christ (1 John 1:7; Heb. 1:3b; Rev. 1:5), whereas the washing that makes us white like wool is a washing of our nature metabolically from within by God's Spirit and by His life (1 Cor. 6:11 and footnote; Titus 3:5 and footnote 4). (Isa. 1:18, footnote 1)

The way to receive God as our salvation is to draw water from the springs of salvation, that is, to drink Him ([Isa. 12:3]; Psa. 36:8; John 4:14; 7:37; 1 Cor. 12:13; Rev. 22:17). To be our salvation, the Triune God was processed to become the life-giving Spirit as the living water, the water of life (1 Cor. 15:45; John 7:37-39; Rev. 21:6; 22:1, 17). When the living water enters into us, it permeates our entire being, causing us to be nourished, transformed, conformed, and glorified (Rom. 12:2; 8:29-30). Both the Old Testament and the New Testament show that God's practical salvation is the processed Triune God Himself as the living water. (Isa. 12:3, footnote 1)

In Isaiah God always considers that He is our salvation as living water ([55:1;] cf. 12:2-3). The record concerning the accomplished redemption in chapter 53 is followed in chapter 55 by the invitation to come to the waters and drink. The call here is like that…in Rev. 22:17. The waters in these two portions of the Word are the redeeming God, the very God who accomplished redemption for us through His incarnation, human living, crucifixion, and resurrection. These waters are both the eternal covenant and the sure mercies shown to David (Isa. 55:3). (Isa. 55:1, footnote 1)

Through all His processes, Christ as the embodiment of the Triune God has accomplished God's full redemption, and now He is applying His complete salvation to His believers.…In totality, what He is and has accomplished is just the divine water, which is the consummated Spirit as the consummation of the Triune God for us to drink and enjoy. (*Life-study of Isaiah*, p. 206)

Further Reading: Life-study of Isaiah, msgs. 30, 40-41

Enlightenment and inspiration: _____

_____

_____

Morning Nourishment

Isa. And in that day Jehovah will punish on high the host
24:21 on high, and the kings of the earth on the earth.
57:15 For thus says the high and exalted One, who inhabits
eternity, whose name is Holy: I will dwell in the high
and holy place, and with the contrite and lowly of
spirit, to revive the spirit of the lowly and to revive
the heart of the contrite.

The first issue of Jehovah's judgment is to unveil Satan's kingdom of darkness (Eph. 6:12b; cf. Dan. 10:13, 20) behind the nations and his oneness with the powers of the nations, such as Nebuchadnezzar as a figure of Satan (Isa. 14:12-15), whom Isaiah regards as one with Satan. According to Daniel 10, there is a prince, a fallen angel, an evil spirit, over every nation. These fallen angels are part of Satan's kingdom of darkness.

The ultimate issue of Jehovah's judgment upon the nations is to provide the all-inclusive Christ as the Savior to meet the need of the beloved Israel and the judged nations. (*Life-study of Isaiah*, pp. 80-81)

Today's Reading

[*Daystar* in Isaiah 14:12] refers to Satan, who, as the Daystar, son of the dawn, was one of the earliest angels (the sons of God—Job 38:7, cf. Job 1:6) created by God at the "dawn" of the universe. He was appointed by God to be the head of all the angels (Ezek. 28:14; Jude 9) and later became Satan, the adversary of God, after he rebelled against God (see footnote 1 on Isa. 14:13). Because of his rebellion, Lucifer as Satan was judged by God (Isa. 14:12-15; Ezek. 28:16-19; Luke 10:18).

In Isaiah 14:12-15 Isaiah identifies Lucifer with Nebuchadnezzar, the king of Babylon (v. 4), thus regarding Nebuchadnezzar as a figure of Satan, as one who was one with Satan (cf. Ezek. 28:12). This unveils Satan's kingdom of darkness behind the nations (Eph. 6:12b; cf. Dan. 10:13, 20) and his oneness with the rulers of the nations. (Isa. 14:12, footnote 1)

Jehovah will punish on high the host on high and the kings of the earth on the earth (Isa. 24:21). Here the host on high refers to

Satan and his angels in the air. Jehovah's reaction will deal both with Satan's army in the air and with the kings on the earth. They will be gathered together like prisoners gathered in a dungeon and will be shut up in prison. After many days they will be punished (v. 22). (*Life-study of Isaiah,* p. 94)

Just as heaven is not God's dwelling place, so the house on earth is not His dwelling place. He looks to a group of people into whom He can enter....[Isaiah 66:1-2 and 57:15] clearly show us that the heavens and the earth are not the dwelling place of God. The dwelling place that God wants to have is a group of people. If God does not gain a group of people, then He will be a God without a home in the universe. Therefore, He longs to gain a group of people so that they can be built together to be His dwelling place.

The whole universe needs a building for God to dwell in man as His abode, and man to dwell in God as his abode. God and man are a mutual abode to each other. Without man, God is a wandering God, a homeless God. In the same way, without God, man is a wandering man, a homeless man.

Therefore, God intends to have a building in this universe in which God is built into man and man is built into God, so that God and man, man and God, can be a mutual abode to each other. First John 4:13 says, "In this we know that we abide in Him and He in us, that He has given to us of His Spirit." Today God is building us into a spiritual house, the temple of God, a universal building, and a universal house, so that God may have a home and man also may have a dwelling place. In this way both God and man may have rest.

The ultimate manifestation of this building is the New Jerusalem. In this city, God is in man, taking man as His dwelling place, and man is in God, having God as his habitation. This is a glorious matter. This is the work God wants to do today. (*The Building Work of God,* pp. 15-18)

Further Reading: Life-study of Isaiah, msg. 12; The Building Work of God, ch. 1

Enlightenment and inspiration: _____

_____

_____

_____

Hymns, #78

1 Gracious Lord, Thy name "I AM" is,
Precious name, how rich and full 'tis,
All-inclusive, faithful too 'tis—
   All we need, Thou art!

2 Thou the Son, the Father in Thee,
As the Spirit now indwell me,
That the riches of Thyself we
   May experience.

3 Thou the Temple for God's dwelling,
Thou the Father's life e'er telling;
We in Thee with joy excelling
   Face to face see Him.

4 Thou the Lamb and Thou the Bridegroom,
For the bride Thou sufferedst sin's doom,
Wounded, crucified in our room;
   Thus we find our rest.

5 Thou art wisdom and the way, Lord,
Thou our lives dost plan each day, Lord,
Grace to us Thou dost convey, Lord,
   In Thy path to walk.

6 Pure and holy, righteous Thou art,
One with God, well-pleasing His heart,
Thou within to us dost impart
   Harmony with God.

7 Thou art life and Thou art light, Lord,
Death hast swallowed, banished night, Lord,
Thou hast quickened, given sight, Lord;
   We are now set free.

8 Thou art resurrection power,
Thou the conqu'ror in hell's hour;
Thou dost us with might empower
   Over all to reign.

9 Living water, food supply, Lord,
Thou Thyself art, and didst die, Lord,
All our want to satisfy, Lord;
   Now we feast on Thee.

10 Thou the Shepherd and Physician,
Thou hast healed our sick condition;
Comfort, guide, protect—Thy mission;
   Thou dost care for us.

11 Priest and King Thou art fore'er, Lord;
    Into God we're brought, and there, Lord,
    Thine authority we share, Lord;
        What an honored place!

12 Thou our Hope and our Redemption,
    Thou wilt change our old creation,
    Make of Thee a duplication,
        Thus Thyself express.

13 Thou our Joy, our Peace, our Glory;
    Truth, and Grace, the Rock, the Life-tree,
    Building, Mountain, Sun, and Shield—we
        Ne'er can tell it all.

14 What Thou art—eternal, boundless,
    Full and perfect, rich, exhaustless—
    Meets our need to utter fullness
        And from us o'erflows.

Composition for prophecy with main point and sub-points: _____

_____

_____

_____

_____

_____

_____

_____

_____

_____

_____

_____

_____

_____

_____

_____

_____

_____

_____

_____

_____

_____

The Age of Restoration
and
Christ as the Shoot of Jehovah
and the Fruit of the Earth

Scripture Reading: Isa. 4:2-6; 2:2-5

Day 1   I. ***In that day*** **in Isaiah 4:2 refers to the coming restoration of the nation of Israel (Matt. 17:11; 19:28; Acts 1:6; 3:21; 15:16):**

A. Basically, between eternity past and eternity future, there are three ages—the age of the old creation, the age of the new creation, and the age of restoration:

1. From God's creation of the heavens and the earth in Genesis 1:1 to the beginning of the age of grace is the age of the old creation.

2. The age of grace is the age of the new creation; the work of God in the age of grace is to produce the new creation (John 1:16-17; 2 Cor. 5:17; Gal. 6:15).

3. The coming age will be the age of restoration (Matt. 19:28; Acts 3:21):

   a. In the coming age God will neither create nor produce the new creation; rather, He will do the work of restoring the old, fallen creation (Rom. 8:20-22).

   b. A restoration will be brought to all things; in this restoration death will be limited, and there will be abundant life and much praise and rejoicing (Isa. 65:18-25).

Day 2   c. After the age of restoration, the entire universe will be changed from the old to the new; then there will be the new heaven and the new earth with the New Jerusalem (v. 17; 66:22; Rev. 21:1-2).

4. Isaiah prophesied concerning the age of restoration (Isa. 2:2-5; 11:1-10; 61:4-9); chapter 35 is a marvelous picture of restoration.

B. God's judgment on the haughty nations ushers in the God-man, Christ (4:2, 5-6), issuing in the restoration of the nation of Israel (vv. 3-6; 2:2-5), which brings in the kingdom and consummates in the new heaven and new earth (65:17).

II. **The all-inclusive Christ is the center and the circumference, the centrality and the universality, of God's eternal economy (Col. 1:15-18):**
  A. As the embodiment of the Triune God, Christ is the reality of every positive thing in the universe (2:16-17).
  B. God's intention in His economy is that Christ be everything; therefore, it is crucial for us to see that God wants nothing but Christ and that in the eyes of God nothing counts except Christ (vv. 16-17; 3:4, 10-11).
  C. Because Christ is the centrality and universality of God's move, the book of Isaiah reveals many aspects of Christ for the fulfillment of God's economy (6:1-8; 22:22; 53:5, 10b-12; 54:5; 55:4-5).

Day 3 III. **In 4:2 there is a pair of aspects of Christ—the Shoot of Jehovah and the Fruit of the earth;** *the Shoot* **is in comparison to** *the Fruit,* **and** *Jehovah* **is in comparison to** *the earth:*
  A. God is eternal, and man came from the earth; *the Fruit of the earth* refers to a man made from dust (Gen. 2:7).
  B. Christ as God came from eternity, but as man He came from the earth, so He is the Shoot of Jehovah and also the Fruit of the earth.

Day 4 IV. *The Shoot of Jehovah* **refers to Christ's deity, showing His divine nature (Isa. 4:2a; John 1:1; 20:28; Rom. 9:5):**
  A. The Shoot of Jehovah typifies not only Christ's divinity but also the sprouting and development of Christ's divinity through the incarnation of God (John 1:1, 14; Heb. 1:1-3; 2:14).
  B. The Shoot of Jehovah is a new development of Jehovah God for the Triune God to branch Himself out for His increase and spreading through His incarnation (Isa. 7:14; Matt. 1:22-23).

C. In His incarnation Christ as the Shoot of Jehovah branched Himself out in His divinity from the territory of divinity into the territory of humanity (John 1:1, 14).

D. In His incarnation Christ came from eternity into time; from ancient times, from the days of eternity, the Triune God was preparing to come forth out of eternity into time, to come with His divinity into humanity (Micah 5:2).

E. The sprouting and development of God in Christ as the Shoot of Jehovah are for the expression of all the riches of divinity in Christ's humanity, that is, for the rich attributes of divinity to be developed into the virtues of Christ, the God-man, in His humanity (Eph. 3:8).

F. The incarnated God, in His divinity, will be the beauty and glory of God's chosen people in the day of restoration (Isa. 4:2a):

1. Our God with His divine nature is our beauty and our glory (60:1, 9, 13).

2. Because Christ lives in us, we are partakers of the divine nature; in this sense, we are not only human but also divine, and the divine nature is our beauty and our glory (Gal. 2:20; 2 Pet. 1:4).

Day 5 V. **The Fruit of the earth refers to Christ's humanity with His human nature (Isa. 4:2b; Luke 1:42):**

A. As the Fruit of the earth, Christ was born a man of human blood and flesh from the earth; the earth was the source of Christ's humanity, just as eternity was the source of His divinity (Heb. 2:14).

B. Christ as the Fruit of the earth is for the multiplication and reproduction of the divine life in humanity (John 12:24):

1. God in Himself, in His divinity, has no way to be multiplied.

2. For His multiplication and reproduction, He needs humanity; humanity is the soil, the earth, for the Triune God to be multiplied and reproduced (20:17; Rom. 8:29; Heb. 2:10).

C. As the Fruit of the earth, Christ, in His humanity, which expresses His divine beauty and glory, will be the excellence and splendor of God's chosen people in the day of restoration (Isa. 4:2b):

1. Even today in the age of grace, we should live a life that expresses Christ's beauty and glory in a divine way and that expresses Christ's excellence and splendor in a human way (1 Cor. 10:31; Phil. 1:11, 20).

2. A proper Christian is both divine and human, having the divine beauty and glory of Jesus and the human excellence and splendor of Jesus (vv. 8-9; 1 Pet. 2:12).

Day 6 VI. **In Isaiah 4:5-6 there is a second pair of aspects of Christ—a covering canopy of glory and an overshadowing tabernacle of grace:**

A. The second pair is the issue of the first pair and is produced by the first pair:

1. Because Christ is the Shoot for God's new development and the Fruit for God's reproduction, He has the divine beauty and glory with the human excellence and splendor; therefore, He can be a canopy covering us and a tabernacle overshadowing us (vv. 2, 5-6).

2. Our Jesus is the God-man, the One who is both divine and human; as the God-man in His divinity and humanity, He, the Shoot of Jehovah and the Fruit of the earth, is a covering canopy of the divine glory and an overshadowing tabernacle of grace in humanity.

B. The God-man, Christ, is a canopy, which is the covering glory of Christ in His divinity that covers all the interests of Jehovah God on earth (v. 5).

C. The overshadowing tabernacle is the God-man, Christ, in His humanity with His grace, as illustrated in 2 Corinthians 12:9; this is Christ as our overshadowing protection and defense (Isa. 4:6; John 1:14).

Morning Nourishment

Acts Whom heaven must indeed receive until the times of
3:21 the restoration of all things, of which God spoke
      through the mouth of His holy prophets from of old.
Isa. But rejoice and exult forever, in what I create, for I
65:18 am now creating Jerusalem as an exultation and her
      people as a rejoicing.

Between eternity past and eternity future there are basically
three ages: the age of the old creation, the age of the new creation,
and the age of restoration. From God's creation of the heavens
and the earth in Genesis 1:1 to the beginning of the age of grace is
the time span of the age of the old creation. The age of grace is the
age of the new creation. Most of the promises in the Old Testament are related to the age of the new creation, the age of grace. A
small portion of the promises in the Old Testament are related to
the coming age such as the ones from Isaiah. In the age of the old
creation God created mankind and the entire universe, and when
what he created became fallen, he came in to heal, to restore. To
restore the fallen creation is to recover and maintain it. God
firstly created and then God restored. We can see from Genesis to
Malachi how God healed, recovered, and maintained His fallen
creation. Part of this maintenance was the keeping of His chosen
people under the custody of the law. (*Elders' Training, Book 5: Fellowship concerning the Lord's Up-to-date Move*, p. 108)

Today's Reading

In the age of grace, God is doing neither a work of creation nor
a work of restoration. The age of grace is the age of the new creation. The old creation is merely the creation without God in it.
The new creation is the old creation born of God with God as its
new element. The old creation, because of the addition of God to it,
becomes the new creation. The old creation does not have the
divine nature, but the new creation, the believers born again of
God, does (John 1:13; 3:15; 2 Peter 1:4). Hence, they are a new creation (Gal. 6:15), not according to the old nature of the flesh, but
according to the new nature of the divine life. The work of God in

the age of grace is to produce the new creation. In the coming age, in the millennium, God will neither create nor produce the new creation, but he will do a work of restoring the old, fallen creation. This restoration work does not include us because by that time we will have become the new creation already.

Acts 3:21 also refers to the times of restoration in the millennium, as prophesied in Isaiah 11:1-10 and 65:18-25, referred to by Christ in Matthew 17:11 and 19:28. Acts 3:21 tells us that heaven must receive the Lord Jesus "until the times of the restoration of all things." The coming age will be an age of restoration. Restoration is not to regenerate with the divine life but to restore the fallen things. According to the Bible, the three ages related to God's work of creation are the age of the old creation, the age of the new creation, and the age of restoration. (*Elders' Training, Book 5: Fellowship concerning the Lord's Up-to-date Move,* pp. 108-109)

According to Isaiah 4:2, the ushering in of Christ will be "in that day,"...the day of the coming restoration of the nation of Israel.

Isaiah 65:18-25 reveals that a restoration will be brought in both to Israel and to all things. Verse 18 says, "Rejoice and exult forever, / In what I create, / For I am now creating Jerusalem as an exultation / And her people as a rejoicing." Jerusalem will be a joy and an exultation, and her people will rejoice. Even God Himself will exult in Jerusalem and rejoice in His people, and there will no longer be heard in her the voice of weeping and of crying (v. 19).

In the restoration, an infant will not die before reaching maturity, and one who dies at the age of a hundred will be regarded as a youth [v. 20]....The unique work carried out by God's people in the restoration will be to sing, praise, worship, and rejoice [vv. 21-22]. ...Calling on the Lord will be their occupation. Even before they call, He will answer [vv. 23-24]....In this restoration death will be limited, and there will be abundant life and much praise and rejoicing [v. 25]. (*Life-study of Isaiah,* pp. 26, 220-221)

Further Reading: Elders' Training, Book 5: Fellowship concerning the Lord's Up-to-date Move, ch. 8; Life-study of Isaiah, msg. 32

Enlightenment and inspiration: _____

_____

_____

Morning Nourishment

Isa.   For I am now creating new heavens and a new earth,
65:17 and the former things will not be remembered, nor
       will they come up in the heart.
Col.   And He is before all things, and all things cohere in
1:17   Him.

At most, the millennium will be a time of restoration. The old
heaven and old earth will be restored during the millennium, but
they will not yet be changed from the old to the new. The changing
of the old heaven and earth into the new heaven and earth will
require another thousand years. Hence, the period of time from
the creation of Adam until the second coming of Christ will issue
in the restoration of the universe, but it will not result in the
renewal of the universe. That will require another thousand
years. After the last thousand years have passed, the entire universe will be changed from the old to the new. Then there will be
the new heaven and the new earth with the New Jerusalem. (*The
Conclusion of the New Testament,* pp. 2594-2595)

Today's Reading

In Isaiah 35 we have a marvelous picture of restoration. The
wilderness and the desert will be glad; and the desert will blossom like the rose. It will blossom and blossom and even exult with
exultation and a ringing shout. The glory of Lebanon will be given
to it, the splendor of Carmel and Sharon; they will see the glory of
Jehovah, the splendor of their God (vv. 1-2). Then the eyes of the
blind will be opened, and the ears of the deaf will be unstopped.
The lame will leap like a hart, and the tongue of the dumb will
give a ringing shout. For water will break forth in the wilderness,
and streams in the desert. The desert mirage will become a pool,
and the thirsty ground, springs of water. In the habitation of jack-
als, their resting place, there will be grass with reeds and rushes.
The place that was once so unpleasant will become the resting
place of the restored people. A highway will be there, and a way,
and it will be called "The Way of Holiness." The unclean will not
pass on it, but it will be for him who walks on the way; no fools will

wander (or err) in it. There will be no lion there, nor will any ravenous animal go up on it. They will not be found there, but the redeemed will walk on it. The ransomed of Jehovah will return and will come to Zion with a ringing shout, and eternal joy will be upon their heads. They will lay hold on gladness and joy, and sorrow and sighing will flee away (vv. 5-10).

Jehovah's humiliating judgment ushers in the God-man, Christ, and issues in the restoration of the nation of Israel. Both the ushering in of Christ and the restoration of Israel come from Jehovah's righteous judgment on the nations. The more God judges the nations, the more Christ is ushered in; and the more Christ is ushered in, the more the restoration of Israel issues out. The ushering in of Christ and the restoration of Israel will result in the millennial kingdom. Finally, the millennium will consummate in the ultimate age of God's economy, that is, in the new heaven and new earth. (*Life-study of Isaiah,* pp. 124, 21)

As the all-inclusive One, Christ is the centrality and universality of God. This expression was first used by Brother Nee in 1934, at the third overcomer conference held in Shanghai. He pointed out from the book of Colossians that the all-inclusive Christ is the center and the circumference of God's purpose. Christ is both the centrality and universality of God's purpose. He is the hub and also the rim. In other words, Christ is all. Again I say that this is not pantheism. It is simply a statement of the fact that Christ is both the center and the circumference of God's economy.

As the embodiment of God, Christ is the reality of every positive thing. Hence, there is no room for Jewish religion or Greek philosophy. There is room only for the all-inclusive Christ. Although Paul was once very strong in Judaism, when he received the revelation concerning Christ, he realized that both Greek philosophy and Jewish tradition were nothing. In God's economy only Christ counts for anything. (*Life-study of Colossians,* pp. 43, 296)

Further Reading: The Conclusion of the New Testament, msgs. 21, 24, 26

__Enlightenment and inspiration:__ _____

_____

_____

Morning Nourishment

Isa. **In that day the Shoot of Jehovah will be beauty and**
4:2 **glory, and the fruit of the earth, excellence and splen-**
    dor, to those of Israel who have escaped.
7:14 **Therefore the Lord Himself will give you a sign:**
    Behold, the virgin will conceive and will bear a son,
    and she will call his name Immanuel.

In Isaiah we can see that our God is an active and aggressive
God. He is moving. He has a personal desire, His heart's pleasure.
Before the foundation of the world He made a plan in Himself.
That plan is His eternal economy to create the universe and man
so that He may have a people to express Him in a marvelous way.
Isaiah's central point is to show us how God made Christ the cen-
trality and universality of His great move for the accomplishment
of His economy. This is why Isaiah reveals so many items of
Christ. Christ has to be many items; otherwise, He could not fulfill God's economy. (*Life-study of Isaiah,* p. 224)

Today's Reading

Isaiah can be considered as a book of poetry, and Hebrew
poetry is composed in pairs. In Isaiah 4:2 there is a pair of aspects
of Christ—the Shoot of Jehovah and the Fruit of the earth. In this
pair there is a comparison. "The Shoot" is in comparison to "the
Fruit," and "Jehovah" is in comparison to "the earth." The title
Immanuel includes "Jehovah" and "the earth" because it means
God with us, that is, God with man. God is eternal, and man came
from the earth. The Fruit of the earth refers to a man made from
the dust (Gen. 2:7). Hebrews 2:14 says that the Lord Jesus shared
in man's blood and flesh. Furthermore, Christ is the eternal God.
John 1:1 says that in the beginning was the Word and the Word
was God. Then verse 14 says that the Word became flesh. Christ
as God came from eternity, but as man He came from the earth, so
He is the Shoot of Jehovah and also the Fruit of the earth.

"The Shoot of Jehovah" indicates that Jehovah is a big tree, a
big plant. The shoot of this plant is a new development for Jehovah to be increased and to spread through His incarnation.

Christ as the Shoot of Jehovah is for the branching out of Jehovah God, in His divinity, into humanity (John 1:14). When Jehovah God branched Himself out, He did it in His divinity to branch Himself into humanity. Before Jesus was born, our unlimited God was existing merely in the territory of His divinity. He did not possess humanity before His incarnation. Approximately two thousand years ago, God was incarnated. In that incarnation, He branched Himself out in His divinity into humanity. From the year of Christ's birth, our God is in both divinity and humanity. This is the difference between the unbelieving Jews' God and our God. Their God is merely in divinity without any element of humanity, but the God we Christians have is One who is in divinity and in humanity. Jesus is the incarnated God, the complete God and the perfect Man.

Jesus was the divine title given by God. Jesus means Jehovah the Savior, or Jehovah the salvation. *Immanuel,* meaning *God with us,* was the name called by man. According to our experience of Jesus, we have to call Him Immanuel, which means God with man. Our Jesus is the God-man. He is both God and man, both divine and human. For God to be in humanity is His spreading, His branching out, from one territory to another territory. Today our God exists in two territories—divinity and humanity. Our God today is both divine and human. (*Life-study of Isaiah,* pp. 224-225)

In eternity God was unlimited. With Him everything was eternal. But when the day of incarnation came, He came out of eternity and entered into time. Eternity has no limit. Time is limited. In eternity He could be everywhere, but in time He could not be in Nazareth when He was in Jerusalem. As a finite man, He was greatly limited....Although the Lord is the eternal, infinite, unlimited God, He lived here on earth as a man, being limited even in the matter of time. As the unlimited God, He entered into the limiting factor of time. (*The Move of God in Man,* p. 13)

Further Reading: Concerning the Person of Christ, pp. 9-14; The Move of God in Man, ch. 1

Enlightenment and inspiration: _____

_____

_____

Morning Nourishment

Micah   But you, O Bethlehem Ephrathah, so little to be
5:2   among the thousands of Judah, from you there
will come forth to Me He who is to be Ruler in
Israel; and His goings forth are from ancient times,
from the days of eternity.
Isa.   Arise! Shine! For your light has come, and the
60:1   glory of Jehovah has risen upon you.

Micah 5:2 is a prophecy concerning Christ. This verse says
that "His goings forth are from ancient times, / From the days
of eternity." His "goings forth" are His coming out. To the
angels it is His going forth, but to us it is His coming out.

"His goings forth are...from the days of eternity" means
that in eternity, before the creation of the earth, Christ was
preparing to come forth. His appearing, His manifestation,
began in eternity. From the ancient times, from the days of
eternity, the Triune God was preparing to come forth out of
eternity into time, to come with His divinity into humanity.
His creation of all things was His preparation to come out of
eternity into time. This was the purpose of creation. Then
while the locusts were operating (Joel 1:4; 2:25), Christ came
forth. In eternity Christ was concealed in His divinity, but
through incarnation He came forth with His divinity into
humanity. (*Life-study of the Minor Prophets,* p. 151)

Today's Reading

The Holy Scriptures, including both the Old Testament
and the New Testament, use various plants, trees, and flow-
ers to signify God.

Isaiah 4:2 says, "In that day the Shoot of Jehovah will be
beauty and glory, and the fruit of the earth, excellence and
splendor, to those of Israel who have escaped." *Shoot* in
Hebrew denotes a new, tender sprout, indicating the initial
development of the growth of a tree. This shows the initial development of the divinity of God in Christ through
incarnation (John 1:14). Christ as the incarnated God is the

shooting forth, the sprouting, of divinity.

The Shoot of Jehovah typifies not only Christ's divinity but the sprouting and development of Christ's divinity through the incarnation of God.

The Shoot of Jehovah is the sprouting of God in Christ. This sprouting comes out of God as the branching out of God Himself for His expression.

The sprouting and development of God in Christ are for the expression of all the riches of divinity in Christ's humanity, that is, for the rich attributes of divinity to be developed into the virtues of Christ, the God-man, in His humanity.

In the development of the divinity in Christ, its sprouting is the beginning of the growth of the divinity in Christ,...[which] will increase until it reaches its goal, that is, the expression of the glory and beauty of divinity.

The development of the divinity in Christ began with His incarnation, in which He was born to be a God-man. Then it passed through His human living on earth for thirty-three and a half years, in which the divine attributes were expressed in His human virtues, and it also passed through His life-releasing death. Eventually, it reached His resurrection, in which He entered into glory.

"That day" in Isaiah 4:2 refers to the day of restoration in the kingdom age. By passing through ascension Christ was made Lord and Christ (Acts 2:33-36), seated on the right hand of the throne of God (Heb. 12:2), and crowned with glory and honor (2:9). In the day that Christ comes back, the consummate development of the divinity in Him will be manifested as beauty and glory; that is, His divinity will be manifested in the brilliant splendor, precious worth, and dignified position in His kingship in His humanity. (*Truth Lessons—Level Three*, vol. 2, pp. 187-188)

Further Reading: Truth Lessons—Level Three, vol. 2, lsn. 37; *The Triune God to Be Life to the Tripartite Man*, ch. 9

Enlightenment and inspiration: _____

_____

_____

Morning Nourishment

Luke 1:42	And she lifted up her voice with a loud cry and said, Blessed are you among women, and blessed is the fruit of your womb!
John 12:24	Truly, truly, I say to you, Unless the grain of wheat falls into the ground and dies, it abides alone; but if it dies, it bears much fruit.

To say that Jesus is the Savior and Redeemer is altogether right, but too shallow. Jesus is not merely our Savior and Redeemer; He is the branching out of God. And He has branched out to us. We all have been caught by Jesus. One day God branched Jesus into us. Eventually this branch bears the fruit. Jesus as a branch is not for a column or beam of a building. Jesus is the branching out of God to bear fruit for our enjoyment. And now we are the branches of Christ to branch out Christ for others' enjoyment. (*The Wonderful Christ in the Canon of the New Testament,* pp. 10-11)

Today's Reading

Jesus today is not only the seed, but also the branch, and this divine branch bears the fruit of the earth....Jesus is the branching out of the Lord into us as the earth. Divinity branches out into our humanity. And through humanity, this branch bears fruit for man's enjoyment...[and] builds God's temple....God's temple is a group of living persons framed together and built up as God's habitation in the spirit....[Only Jesus] can build this temple...by being the seed, the branch, and the fruit.

Hence, Jesus as the seed is the branching out of God to bear fruit for our enjoyment. This seed will also bruise the head of the serpent, and in this seed shall all the nations be blessed. It is the branching out of this seed that will build God's temple, and it is this branch that bears the priesthood and the kingship. "Indeed, it is he who will build the temple of Jehovah; and he will bear majesty and will sit and rule on his throne; and he will be a priest on his throne; and the counsel of peace will be between the two of them" (Zech. 6:13). (*The Wonderful Christ in the Canon of the New Testament,* p. 11)

Christ is...the Fruit of the earth (Isa. 4:2b). When Mary came to Elizabeth, Elizabeth said to Mary, "Blessed are you among women, and blessed is the fruit of your womb!" (Luke 1:42). The fruit in the womb of Mary was Jesus. He was in her womb as the Fruit of the earth.

As the Fruit of the earth, Christ was a man born of human blood and flesh from the earth (Heb. 2:14). The earth is the source of Christ's humanity, just as eternity is the source of His divinity.

Christ as the Fruit of the earth is for the multiplication and reproduction of the divine life in humanity (John 12:24). God in Himself, in His divinity, has no way to be multiplied. Christ as the Fruit of the earth is for multiplication. He was a grain of wheat who died so that many grains could be produced. For His multiplication and reproduction, He needed humanity. Humanity is the soil, the earth, for the Triune God to be multiplied and reproduced.

Such a man, the Man Jesus, in His humanity, which expresses His divine beauty and glory, will be the excellence and splendor of God's chosen people in the day of restoration. Even today in the age of grace, we need to experience the excellence and splendor of Jesus in His humanity. On the one hand, a proper Christian should have the divine beauty and glory of Jesus. On the other hand, he should also have the human excellence and splendor of Jesus. A Christian must be both divine and human. Our own human excellence and splendor are very low, but when we live Christ, the human excellence and splendor which we live out are very high. We must live a life which expresses Christ's beauty and glory in a divine way and which expresses Christ's excellence and splendor in a human way. We may not realize much of this today, but when the time of restoration comes, those of us who overcome will be raptured, transformed, and glorified. Then we will fully realize that we have the divine beauty and glory of Jesus and the human excellence and splendor of Jesus. (*Life-study of Isaiah*, pp. 226-227)

Further Reading: The Wonderful Christ in the Canon of the New Testament, chs. 1, 19

Enlightenment and inspiration: _____

_____

_____

_____

Morning Nourishment

Isa. **Jehovah will create over the entire region of Mount**
4:5-6 **Zion and over all her convocations a cloud of smoke**
by day, and the brightness of a fiery flame by night;
for the glory will be a canopy over all. And there will
be a tabernacle as a daytime shade from the heat and
as a refuge and a cover from storm and rain.

There are two pairs of what Christ is in Isaiah 4. The first pair is
the Shoot of Jehovah and the Fruit of the earth. The second pair is
in verses 5 and 6 where Christ is seen as a covering canopy of glory
and an overshadowing tabernacle of grace. The second pair is the
issue of the first pair and is produced by the first pair. The canopy is
covering, and the tabernacle is overshadowing. The canopy is of the
divine glory, and the tabernacle is of Christ's grace in His humanity. When Christ was incarnated, He was full of grace and the disciples beheld His glory (John 1:14). (*Life-study of Isaiah,* p. 227)

Today's Reading

The Shoot of Jehovah and the Fruit of the earth, as the God-
man in His divinity and His humanity as well, will be a covering
canopy of the divine glory and an overshadowing tabernacle of
grace in humanity.

Christ as a covering canopy of glory is the divine glory covering all the interests of Jehovah God in His holy mountain (Isa.
4:5). The holy mountain is Mount Zion. God's temple was on
Mount Zion, and God's people were there having all kinds of convocations. These convocations, these meetings of God's people,
were the interests of God on the earth. God's interests on the
earth need such a covering canopy of glory.

When the day of restoration comes, there will be over Mount
Zion a cloud of smoke in the day and the brightness of a fiery flame
in the night....God's glory as the cloud of smoke and the brightness of the fiery flame will remain on Mount Zion all the time. In
the day His glory will be as a covering cloud of smoke to be a shade
from the heat. In the night His glory will be as the shining brightness of a fiery flame to keep God's people away from darkness.

God Himself as the glory expressed in Christ will remain as a canopy over Mount Zion to cover His interests, which include His holy temple, His holy people, and all His holy convocations.

Christ will also be an overshadowing tabernacle of grace in humanity (Isa. 4:6, John 1:14)....This overshadowing tabernacle of grace is Christ in His humanity, which expresses His divinity (John 1:14b)....He is presently overshadowing His believers in His grace as a daytime shade from the heat and as a refuge and a cover from storm and rain (2 Cor. 12:9). Christ is the canopy to cover God's interests, and He is also a tabernacle to be our shade and our refuge. The tabernacle is a shade, a refuge, and a cover. Our experience of this is fully explained in 2 Corinthians 12:9, which describes Christ overshadowing His believers in His grace as their strength. The Shoot of Jehovah and the Fruit of the earth are one pair of items of Christ in Isaiah 4. This pair produces another pair—Christ as a covering canopy of glory and an over-shadowing tabernacle of grace in humanity.

According to Isaiah 4, our Christ is the new development of God. He is the branching out of God in His divinity into humanity. As such a One, He will be the beauty and glory of God's chosen people in the day of restoration. This glory will be a great canopy to cover all of God's interests on earth. Christ is also the Fruit of the earth for the multiplication and reproduction of the divine life in humanity. This reproducing Fruit of the earth will be the excellence and splendor of God's chosen people. Christ is also a shade to us from the heat and a refuge and a cover to protect us from the storm and rain. Have we ever considered that Christ is so many items in Isaiah 4? Christ is God's development, God's branching out, and the Fruit for God's reproduction; He has the divine beauty and glory with the human excellence and splendor. Therefore, He can cover us as a canopy and overshadow us as a tabernacle to be our shade and refuge. Isaiah 4 shows that Christ is everything to us. (*Life-study of Isaiah*, pp. 228-230)

Further Reading: Life-study of Isaiah, msg. 33

Enlightenment and inspiration: _____

_____

_____

Hymns, #496

1   Christ is the one reality of all,
    Of Godhead and of man and all things else;
    No man without Him ever findeth God,
    Without Him man and everything is false.

2   All types and figures of the ancient time,
    All things we ever need, both great and small,
    Only are shadows of the Christ of God,
    Showing that He must be our all in all.

3   All things are vanity of vanities,
    Christ, the reality all things to fill;
    Though everything we may enjoy and own,
    If we're devoid of Christ we're empty still.

4   Christ is our real God, our real Lord,
    Christ is our real life, our real light;
    Christ is our real food, our real drink,
    Our real clothing, and our real might.

5   Christ also is the one reality
    Of all our doctrine and theology;
    And all our scriptural knowledge without Him
    Is just in letter and is vanity.

6   Christ, the reality of time and space,
    Christ, the reality of every stage;
    Christ is the one reality of all
    Thru all eternity from age to age.

Composition for prophecy with main point and sub-points: _____

The Vision of Christ in Glory

Scripture Reading: Isa. 6:1-8; John 12:38-41

Day 1
&
Day 2

I. **"In the year that King Uzziah died I saw the Lord sitting on a high and lofty throne, and the train of His robe filled the temple" (Isa. 6:1):**

A. The One who was seen by Isaiah was Christ as the Lord, the King, Jehovah of hosts (v. 5b):

1. John, in his account of Christ's living and working on earth, said that Isaiah "saw His glory and spoke concerning Him" (John 12:41).

2. In order to see the vision of the glorious enthroned Christ, we need to take heed to Isaiah's warning word (Isa. 6:9-10) by exercising our spirit to pray that the Lord would open our inner eyes, soften our heart, and keep our heart turned to Him so that we may receive His inner healing of our blindness and sickness (John 12:38-40; Matt. 13:14-17; Acts 28:25-27; Rev. 3:18; 4:2; 2 Cor. 3:16-18).

2Cor3:16-18 shows, that as The Spirit the Lord is in us we can behold Him & reflect Him.

Warning of Isa.

B. The vision of Christ in glory was seen by Isaiah in his *We have to Pray Prre.* depression (Isa. 6:1, 5; cf. 22:1; 2 Chron. 26:3-5, 16-22):

1. In spite of the rebellion, iniquities, and corruptions of God's chosen and beloved people, Christ is still sitting on a high and lofty throne in glory (Isa. 6:1-4; Lam. 5:19; Rev. 22:1).

2. Christ is the unique good thing in the universe; we must look at Him with undivided attention by turning away from every other object; we should not look at anything or anyone other than Christ (Heb. 12:1-2a).

3. On this earth everything changes and fluctuates, but Christ remains the same today and forever; hence, we should not look down at the situation on earth but should look up to Christ on the throne (v. 2; 13:8).

C. Christ's long robe signifies His splendor in His virtues, expressed mainly in and through His humanity;

that Christ was wearing a long robe indicates that He appeared to Isaiah in the image of a man; Christ is the enthroned God-man with the divine glory expressed in His human virtues (Isa. 6:1; cf. Ezek. 1:26, 22; Acts 2:36; Heb. 2:9a).

II. **"Seraphim hovered over Him, each having six wings: With two he covered his face, and with two he covered his feet, and with two he flew. And one called to the other, saying: Holy, holy, holy, Jehovah of hosts; / The whole earth is filled with His glory" (Isa. 6:2-3):**

A. Isaiah saw the long robe signifying Christ's splendor in His virtues, and the seraphim were praising Christ in His holiness and declaring that the whole earth is filled with Christ's glory.

B. Isaiah saw Christ in His divine glory with His human virtues and His holiness based on His righteousness:

1. The seraphim signify or represent the holiness of Christ, the embodiment of the Triune God; they were standing there for Christ's holiness.

2. Christ's holiness is based on His righteousness; because Christ was always righteous, He was sanctified, separated, from the common people (5:16).

Day 3 III. **"And the foundations of the threshold shook at the voice of him who called, and the house was filled with smoke. Then I said, Woe is me, for I am finished! / For I am a man of unclean lips, / And in the midst of a people of unclean lips I dwell; / Yet my eyes have seen the King, Jehovah of hosts" (6:4-5):**

A. The shaking of the foundations of the threshold signifies solemnity, and the house being filled with smoke signifies glory burning in awe (cf. 4:5).

B. As a result of seeing this vision, Isaiah was terminated, finished, realizing that he was a man of

unclean lips, dwelling in the midst of a people
of unclean lips (6:5):

1. Revelation comprises seeing as well as killing; the greatest thing in the Christian experience is the killing that comes from light.
2. The more we see God, the more we see what
   we are and the more we deny ourselves and
   hate ourselves (Job 42:5-6; Psa. 36:9; Eph.
   5:13; Luke 5:8).
3. Everyone who truly sees a vision of the Lord
   in His glory is enlightened in his conscience
   concerning his uncleanness (cf. v. 8).
4. A great percentage of the words that we speak
   are evil because most of the words are words
   of criticism; if we eliminate gossip, murmuring, and reasoning, we may find that we have
   very little to talk about (Phil. 2:12-14; cf. Luke
   6:45; Eph. 4:29-30; 1 Pet. 1:15-16).

Day 4   C. How much we realize concerning ourselves
          depends upon how much we see the Lord; for this
          reason we need a revival every morning; morning
          revival is the time for us to see the Lord (Matt. 5:8;
          Psa. 27:4, 8).

          D. The more we see the Lord and are measured by
          the Lord, the more we are cleansed, supplied, and
          transformed (Ezek. 40:3; 47:3-5).

          E. Seeing God transforms us because in seeing God,
          we gain God and receive His element into us (2 Cor.
          3:18).

Day 5   IV. **"Then one of the seraphim flew to me with an
          ember in his hand, which he had taken from
          the altar with a pair of tongs. And he touched
          my mouth with it and said, Now that this has
          touched your lips, / Your iniquity is taken away,
          and your sin is purged" (Isa. 6:6-7):**

          A. After Isaiah realized that he was unclean, he was
          purged by one of the seraphim, signifying the holi-
          ness of God (v. 6a).

          B. Isaiah was purged with an ember from the altar;

the application of this ember by the seraphim
signifies the effectiveness of Christ's redemption
accomplished on the cross and applied by "the
Spirit, the Holy" in His judging, burning, and
sanctifying power (vv. 6b-7a; 4:4; cf. Luke 12:49;
Rev. 4:5).

C. This purging by the seraphim with an ember from
the altar took away Isaiah's iniquity and purged
his sin (Isa. 6:7b).

Day 6   V. **"Then I heard the voice of the Lord, saying,
Whom shall I send? Who will go for Us? And
I said, Here am I; send me" (v. 8; cf. John 17:21;
20:21-22):**

A. Seeing God issues in being purged and cleansed
by God, and being cleansed by God issues in being
sent by God (Isa. 6:6-8; 1 John 1:7-9).

B. The words *I* and *Us* indicate that the One speak-
ing is triune and that this One is not merely
Christ but Christ as the embodiment of the
Triune God (Isa. 6:8a; Col. 2:9).

C. The Triune God sends us to bring His chosen
people into a state of living Christ so that they
might express Him in His glory, be saturated with
His holiness, and live in His righteousness (Isa.
6:8b; Acts 13:47; Isa. 49:6; Phil. 1:21a).

Morning Nourishment

Isa. **In the year that King Uzziah died I saw the Lord sit-**
6:1 **ting on a high and lofty throne, and the train of His**
robe filled the temple.
5 **...My eyes have seen the King, Jehovah of hosts.**
Rev. **...He showed me a river of water of life, bright as crystal,**
22:1 **proceeding out of the throne of God and of the Lamb...**

In spite of the rebellion, iniquities, and corruptions of Israel, His chosen and beloved people, Christ is still sitting on a high and lofty throne in glory (Isa. 6:1-4). These verses indicate that no matter what the situation might be on earth and regardless of the corruption and degradation among God's people, Christ is still on the throne in His glory.

When Isaiah looked at the situation among the children of Israel, he became very disappointed. For this reason, in the first five chapters of his prophecy, he had very little to say that was good about the children of Israel. It was at this point that the Lord brought him into a vision so that he could see the Lord of glory sitting on the throne (v. 1). The Lord seemed to say to Isaiah, "Don't look down at the situation. If you look down, you will be disappointed. Look up at Me. I am still here. There may be nothing good there, but everything is good here. I am the unique good thing in the universe. Look at Me."

Therefore, in the church life, we need to learn not to look down at the situation but to look up to Christ. We should not look at anything or anyone other than Christ. The Christ whom we look up to is no longer on the cross; today Christ is on the throne.

The people had become fallen, but Christ and His throne remained the same in His glory (v. 1a). On this earth, everything changes and fluctuates, but Christ remains the same today and forever (Heb. 13:8). (*Life-study of Isaiah*, pp. 35-36)

Today's Reading

The train of Christ's robe still filled the temple (Isa. 6:1b). Christ's long robe signifies Christ's splendor in His virtues. Whereas glory refers mainly to God, splendor refers mainly to man. The splendor of Christ in His virtues is expressed mainly in and through His humanity.

We may desire to go to heaven to see Christ's glory in His divinity, but in Isaiah's vision this Christ in glory is full of splendor in His human virtues. When we see Christ in His glory, we will see Him mainly in His humanity, which is full of virtues. All Christ's virtues are bright and shining, and this shining is His splendor. Christ's glory is in His divinity, and His splendor is in His humanity.

Isaiah loved God and loved Israel, God's elect. He realized by looking at Israel's situation, that there was not the expression of God's glory. Israel had also violated God's holiness and had become corrupt in human virtues. Furthermore, King Uzziah had died. Among the kings of Israel, he was a very good king, yet he died. In that kind of environment, Isaiah was surely very depressed. The Lord appeared to him in his depression.

In Isaiah 6 Christ, the God-man, is seen in His divine glory. This God-man is unveiled in chapter four as the Shoot of Jehovah, the Fruit of the earth, a canopy covering God's interests in the entire universe, and the tabernacle overshadowing God's elect to protect them from all kinds of troubles. Isaiah 6 shows us the same One in another aspect. In Isaiah 6 He is the God in glory sitting on the throne. Because He is wearing a long robe, He is also a man. This One is the God-man with divine glory and human virtues.

His human virtues are signified by the long train of His robe. This indicates that the vision here pays more attention to Christ's human virtues. The four Gospels show us Christ as God and as man, but...we see more of Christ in His manhood and in His humanity than in His divinity. Christ is expressed in His human virtues much more than in His divine glory. However, His human virtues need the divine glory as a source. Christ is a person with the divine glory expressed in His human virtues. (*Life-study of Isaiah*, pp. 36-37, 235-236)

Further Reading: Life-study of Isaiah, msg. 6

Enlightenment and inspiration: _____

_____

_____

_____

Morning Nourishment

Isa. Seraphim hovered over Him, each having six wings:
6:2-3 With two he covered his face, and with two he covered his feet, and with two he flew. And one called
to the other, saying: Holy, holy, holy, Jehovah of hosts;
the whole earth is filled with His glory.

John These things said Isaiah because he saw His glory and
12:41 spoke concerning Him.

We all have to see the full vision of Christ in Isaiah 6. Christ is sitting on a high and lofty throne as the Lord, the King, Jehovah of hosts. He is the very God on the throne. John the apostle told us in John 12 that Isaiah saw Christ's glory. This means that Jehovah of hosts, the King, the Lord, was Christ. Christ was wearing a long robe in this vision. This means that Christ's humanity is "long." The train of Christ's robe fills the temple. The Lord who appeared to Isaiah was on a high and lofty throne in His divine glory (John 12:39-41), signified by the smoke, and with His human virtues, signified by the train of His robe. His holiness is held by the seraphim (Isa. 6:2-3).

Christ is seen in Isaiah 6 as God in His divinity, signified by the smoke, and as a man in His humanity, signified by the train of His robe.

Christ's divine glory is filling the earth (Isa. 6:3b), whereas His human virtues are filling the temple (v. 1b). The glory filling the earth is universal, and the robe filling the temple is local. (*Life-study of Isaiah,* pp. 236-237)

Today's Reading

In Isaiah 6…Christ is seen in His divine glory with His human virtues held in His holiness. His glory is divine, His virtues are human, and His holiness is standing fast. The Bible says that no man has seen God at any time (John 1:18a). Our God is invisible, yet Isaiah saw Him. Isaiah declared that he saw the Lord, the King, Jehovah of hosts (Isa. 6:1).

A clear picture is presented in Isaiah 6, showing us Christ in glory. This chapter, however, does not give us a detailed description of what Christ looks like. Isaiah only says, "In the year that King Uzziah died I saw the Lord sitting on a high and lofty throne, and the train of His robe filled the temple" (v. 1). The Lord seen by Isaiah must have been in the image of a man because verse 1 tells us that the train of His robe filled the temple. His robe is the first main item in this scene because it fills the temple. The second main item in Isaiah's vision is the temple being filled with smoke (v. 4). The third main item is the seraphim (v. 2). Verse two says, "Seraphim hovered over Him, each having six wings." The word "hovered" literally means "stood." The seraphim stood over Him. We know that they were standing for His holiness because they declare, "Holy, holy, holy, Jehovah of hosts" (v. 3). Verse 4 says, "The foundations of the threshold shook at the voice of him who called." The divine glory is another major item in Isaiah's vision. Verse 3 says, "The whole earth is filled with His glory." John 12 says that Isaiah saw the Lord's glory and spoke concerning Him (v. 41). The smoke that filled the house, the temple, in Isaiah 6:4 is the glory. Isaiah 4:5 also refers to glory as a cloud of smoke over the convocations of Israel.

The divine glory is signified by the smoke, holiness is signified by the seraphim, and the Lord's human virtues are signified by the train of His robe. Human virtues mainly are based upon righteousness. An unrighteous person does not have human virtues. He is bankrupt in human virtues because he is unrighteous. Human virtues depend upon righteousness. When Christ accomplished His redemption on the cross, He fulfilled the requirements of God's glory, God's holiness, and God's righteousness. As fallen sinners, we cannot fulfill the requirements of God's glory, holiness, and righteousness, but Christ satisfied them. We need to see the vision of Christ in Isaiah 6 in His glory, His holiness, and His righteousness with His human virtues. (*Life-study of Isaiah,* pp. 234-235)

Further Reading: Life-study of Isaiah, msg. 34

Enlightenment and inspiration: _____

_____

_____

Morning Nourishment

Isa. And the foundations of the threshold shook at the
6:4-5 voice of him who called, and the house was filled with
smoke. Then I said, Woe is me, for I am finished! For
I am a man of unclean lips, and in the midst of a people of unclean lips I dwell; yet my eyes have seen the
King, Jehovah of hosts.

In Isaiah 6:4 we see that the foundations of the threshold
shook at the voice of him who called. This shaking signifies solemnity. In this verse we also see that the house was filled with
smoke. This signifies glory burning in awe.

In Isaiah 6:5 we have the response of Isaiah....Isaiah responded to the vision of Christ in glory by saying, "Woe is me, for I am
finished!" (v. 5a). As a result of seeing this vision, Isaiah was terminated, finished.

Isaiah went on to say, "For I am a man of unclean lips, / And in
the midst of a people of unclean lips I dwell" (v. 5b). By this we can
see that we must pay attention to our lips, to our speaking. Every
day we talk too much. A great percentage of the words we speak
are evil, because most of our words are words of criticism. Nearly
every word that we speak concerning any matter or any person is
a word of criticism. This is the reason that our lips are unclean.
Unclean things such as gossip, murmuring, and reasoning make
the church life taste like vinegar. If we eliminate gossip, murmuring, and reasoning, we may find that we have very little to talk
about. Like Isaiah, we need to realize that our lips are unclean.

Everyone who truly sees a vision of the Lord is enlightened.
The vision he sees immediately exposes him and brings him into
light. When Peter saw the Lord in Luke 5, he immediately said to
the Lord, "Depart from me, for I am a sinful man, Lord." (v. 8).
(*Life-study of Isaiah*, pp. 37-38)

Today's Reading

After you were saved, perhaps you knelt down by your bed to
pray one morning; you came before God and touched Him. At that
time it seemed as if someone descended from heaven to judge

your lips and tongue, saying, "Your lips are so filthy, and your tongue is so sharp." Your lips and tongue were judged by God. When God's light judged you, you reproved and judged yourself, saying, "My lips are indeed filthy, and my tongue is indeed sharp." This is the same as what happened in Isaiah 6:5 when Isaiah met God in a vision....You met God, and your lips and tongue were judged. Then you went on to pray, "Lord, my lips are filthy. Cleanse me with Your blood so that my lips and tongue will be consecrated to You and placed at Your disposal from now on." From that point on, your lips and tongue were separated. If you utter frivolous or sharp words, you will feel uneasy inside. You can no longer speak so freely, because your lips and tongue have been consecrated to God.

Wherever there is judgment and measuring, there is the outflow of the water of life. Often you are powerless in preaching the gospel because your lips and tongue have not been measured; consequently, the water of life cannot flow out from your lips and tongue. When you are enlightened, judged, and measured by God, the water of life will flow out from you. Just one measurement, however, is not adequate; God will measure you two, three, and many times. God measures your lips and tongue first, and then He may measure your clothing and adornments. After you are measured by God, others will sense that even your hair and clothing are dripping with the water of life. Your clothing will satisfy those who are inwardly thirsty, refresh those who are inwardly dry, and illumine those who are inwardly dark, because your clothing has been judged, measured, and sanctified by God. How much the water of life flows out depends on how much God has gained you. As God gains more of you, the water of life will flow farther and deeper. Whether or not the water will flow far or deep enough depends on how much you are measured by God. (*The Collected Works of Watchman Nee*, vol. 38, pp. 469-470)

Further Reading: The Collected Works of Watchman Nee, vol. 50, ch. 36; vol. 38, ch. 61

Enlightenment and inspiration: _____

_____

_____

_____

Morning Nourishment

Job   I had heard of You by the hearing of the ear, but now
42:5-6 my eye has seen You; therefore I abhor *myself,* and I
        repent in dust and ashes.
Luke   And when Simon Peter saw *this,* he fell down at
5:8   Jesus' knees, saying, Depart from me, for I am a sinful
        man, Lord.

How much we realize concerning ourselves depends on how
much we see the Lord. For this reason, we need a revival every
morning. The morning revival is the time for us to see the Lord
again. The more we see the Lord, the more we see what we are.
We realize that there is nothing good within us and that everything within us is without splendor or virtue.

Although Isaiah knew that he was finished and that he was a
man of unclean lips, he nevertheless knew that he had seen the
King, Jehovah of hosts, with his eyes (Isa. 6:5c). (*Life-study of Isaiah,* p. 38)

Today's Reading

Light exposes our true condition. The self that we see today is
thousands of times more evil and filthy than the self that we spoke
of in the past. Under such circumstances, our pride, self, and flesh
will wilt away. They will be removed and no longer survive.

The wonderful thing is that whatever we see under the light is
killed by the light....When we see our shortcomings under the shining, the shortcomings are finished immediately; they are killed
immediately. Light kills; this is the most wonderful thing about
the Christian experience. As the Holy Spirit enlightens us, we are
dealt with. Therefore, revelation comprises seeing as well as killing. Through seeing, the flesh withers away. Revelation is God's
way of operation. In fact, revelation is God's operation itself. As
soon as light reveals, it kills. When light shines, we see, and our seeing kills everything. Once we see how filthy and evil something is
and see the Lord's condemnation of it, it can no longer survive.

The greatest thing in the Christian experience is the killing
that comes from light. Paul did not receive a shining and then

hasten to kneel beside the road; the very instant he was enlightened, he fell down. Prior to that, he was able to plan for everything, and he was confident about everything. However, his first reaction when the light came was to fall down. He became foolish and ignorant. Light brought him down. We should take note that these two things happen as one step, not two steps. It does not happen the way we think....God does not enlighten us concerning our shortcomings, and then we begin to change these shortcomings. No, God does not work this way. He shows us how evil, filthy, and short we are, and as soon as we see this, we exclaim, "My! What a filthy and evil man I am!" As soon as God shows us our true condition, we fall. We wither away and are not able to stand up any longer. Once a proud man is enlightened, he is no longer able to be proud even if he tries. Once we have seen our true condition under God's light and once we have seen what our pride is, the impression will never leave us. Something will remain in us that will give us pain, that will give us the feeling that we are useless, and we will no longer be able to be proud.

As soon as the Lord shines on us, we have to fall under His light and say, "Lord, I accept Your judgment. I accept Your view." If we do this, God will give us more light and will show us how filthy we are.

Under God's shining, we find out the kind of person we are. As soon as God's revelation comes, our condition is exposed and laid bare. He exposes us, and we see ourselves. Previously, only the Lord knew us. We were naked and laid bare before Him, but not before ourselves; we still did not know ourselves. But when God exposes all of the thoughts and intentions of the heart to us, we become naked not only before Him, but before ourselves as well. ...We prostrate before the Lord and repent, saying, "I repent of myself. I hate myself. I admit that I am an incurable man." (Watchman Nee, *The Breaking of the Outer Man and the Release of the Spirit*, pp. 96-99)

Further Reading: The Breaking of the Outer Man and the Release of the Spirit, ch. 8; Life-study of Job, msg. 30

Enlightenment and inspiration: _____
_____
_____

Morning Nourishment

Isa. Then one of the seraphim flew to me with an ember in
6:6-7 his hand, *which* he had taken from the altar with a
pair of tongs. And he touched my mouth *with it* and
said, Now that this has touched your lips, your iniquity is taken away, and your sin is purged.

4:4 When the Lord has washed away the filth of the daughters of Zion and has cleansed away the bloodstains of
Jerusalem from her midst, by the judging Spirit and
the burning Spirit.

Psa. For with You is the fountain of life; in Your light we
36:9 see light.

This shining, repentance, shame, loathing, and prostration
will shake off what we have been unable to shake off all these
years. Man's salvation comes from this instant enlightening.
The seeing and removing are one work; the two are joined
together. As the Lord shines, He saves. The shining is the saving,
and the seeing is the deliverance. We need this kind of seeing
before the Lord. Only this kind of shining will remove our pride,
and only this light will stop our fleshly activities and break our
outer shell. (Watchman Nee, *The Breaking of the Outer Man and
the Release of the Spirit,* p. 99)

Today's Reading

[Leviticus 12:2 says, "If a woman conceives seed and bears a
male child, then she shall be unclean seven days."] In figure the
woman represents all mankind (see footnote 1 on Genesis 3:2).
Thus, the uncleanness within the woman signifies the uncleanness within all mankind. Since the source is unclean, whatever
is born of the source must also be unclean. All mankind was born
in uncleanness (Psa. 51:5) and consequently lives in uncleanness (Eph. 2:1-3; 4:17-19). In Leviticus 11 the uncleanness is outside of man, but in chapter 12 the uncleanness is within man
(cf. Matt. 15:17-20; Rom. 5:19a). (Lev. 12:2, footnote 1)

Isaiah 6:6-7 speaks concerning the purging of Isaiah....After

Isaiah realized that he was unclean, he was purged by one of the
seraphim, signifying the holiness of God (v. 6a)....Isaiah was
purged with an ember from the altar (vv. 6b-7a). This ember signifies the effectiveness of Christ's redemption accomplished on
the cross....This purging by the seraphim with an ember from
the altar took away Isaiah's iniquity and purged his sin (v. 7b).

Had Isaiah not been washed by God before his experience in
chapter six? Yes, Isaiah had been cleansed, but he realized that
he was still unclean. This indicates that we all need to realize
that we are a totality of uncleanness. No matter how many
times we may be washed, we are still unclean. We all must come
to know ourselves to this extent.

In our experience, whether we are clean or unclean depends
on the feeling of our conscience, and the feeling of our conscience
depends on our seeing the Lord. How much we see the Lord de-
termines how much we will be cleansed. The more we see the
Lord and are exposed, the more we are cleansed. When our conscience is cleansed and is void of offense, we are able to contact
God. According to our enlightened conscience, we are clean, but
according to the actual facts of our situation in the old creation,
we are not clean. How could the old creation be clean? As long as
we remain in the old creation, we can never be completely clean,
for the old creation is unclean. We need the redemption of our
body. Once our body is redeemed, we will get out of the old creation. At that time, we will be completely clean. (*Life-study of
Isaiah*, pp. 38-39)

Everyone who truly sees a vision of the Lord in His glory
is enlightened in his conscience regarding his uncleanness
(cf. Luke 5:8). (Isa. 6:5, footnote 1)

The ember from the altar [in Isaiah 6:6] signifies the effectiveness of Christ's redemption accomplished on the cross. (Isa.
6:6, footnote 1)

Further Reading: The Crucial Revelation of Life in the Scriptures,
    ch. 5

Enlightenment and inspiration: _____

Morning Nourishment

Isa. Then I heard the voice of the Lord, saying, Whom
6:8 shall I send? Who will go for Us? And I said, Here am I;
send me.

John That they all may be one; even as You, Father, are in
17:21 Me and I in You, that they also may be in Us; that the
world may believe that You have sent Me.

20:21-22 Then Jesus said to them again, Peace be to you; as the
Father has sent Me, I also send you. And when He had
said this, He breathed into *them* and said to them,
Receive the Holy Spirit.

After Isaiah was purged, he received a commission from
the Lord [Isaiah 6:8-13]....Regarding the Lord's need, we first
have His calling. The Lord said, "Whom shall I send? Who will
go for Us?" (v. 8a). The words *I* and *Us* indicate that the One
speaking here is triune, that this One is not merely Christ
but Christ as the embodiment of the Triune God....Isaiah's
answer was very good. He said, "Here am I; send me" (v. 8b).
(*Life-study of Isaiah*, pp. 39-40)

Today's Reading

Isaiah 6:8-10 shows us Isaiah being sent. He was sent by
the Christ who is full of the divine glory and the human virtues in His holiness (vv. 1-4). Christ's holiness is based upon
His righteousness. Isaiah 5:16 says, "Jehovah of hosts is
exalted in judgment, / And the holy God shows Himself holy in
righteousness." God is sanctified in His righteousness. Someone who is righteous is separated from the common people. A
righteous person is a sanctified person. He is not common but
holy, separated unto God. Righteousness is the foundation of
God's throne (Psa. 97:2), and we are expecting new heavens
and a new earth in which righteousness dwells (2 Pet. 3:13).
Since God is righteous, He is holy, sanctified, separated from
the common people. In the four Gospels, Jesus surely was a
separated, unique, and particular person because He was
righteous all the time. Therefore, He is holy, sanctified.

Isaiah was sent by Christ to a people who were short of the divine glory, were violating the divine holiness, and were corrupt in the human virtues (Isa. 6:5). He was sent by the Lord to lead Israel to express Christ's divine glory in His human virtues held in His holiness (Isa. 5:16b). In other words, God wanted Israel to be a holy people, fully separated from the nations. Their holiness is based upon their righteousness. Then they could express God's glory. Today, to live Christ is to express God's glory. To live Christ is to be righteous. Righteousness is the base, the foundation, of God's salvation. God's salvation firstly justifies us, making us righteous. Then we will be holy, sanctified, separated. Spontaneously, we will be brought into the expression of the divine glory of Christ, which is to live Christ.

Every sent one is sent by the Lord to do the same thing. First, God sent the prophets. Second, God sent His Son. Third, God sent the New Testament apostles. He sent them all to bring God's chosen people into a state of living Christ. He desired that they would live righteousness, showing that they are a holy people, different and distinct from the nations. Then they would express Christ's divine glory. To live Christ is to express Christ's divine glory in His holiness with His righteousness. We must be righteous people, holy people, and people full of the divine glory. Then we will be those who live Christ. (*Life-study of Isaiah,* pp. 237-238)

The Lord sent His disciples with Himself as life and everything to them. (See footnote 1 on John 17:18.) This is why, immediately after He said, "I also send you" [20:21], He breathed the Holy Spirit into them [v. 22]. By His breathing into them He entered as the Spirit into the disciples to abide in them forever (14:16-17). Hence, wherever His disciples were sent, He was always with them. He was one with them. (John 20:21, footnote 2)

Further Reading: Life-study of Isaiah, msg. 34

Enlightenment and inspiration: _____

_____

_____

_____

Hymns, #505

1   There's a Man in the glory
      Whose Life is for me.
    He's pure and He's holy,
      Triumphant and free.
    He's wise and He's loving,
      How tender is He!
    His Life in the glory,
      My life must be;
    His Life in the glory,
      My life must be.

2   There's a Man in the glory
      Whose Life is for me.
    He overcame Satan;
      From bondage He's free.
    In Life He is reigning;
      How kingly is He!
    His Life in the glory,
      My life must be;
    His Life in the glory,
      My life must be.

3   There's a Man in the glory
      Whose Life is for me.
    In Him is no sickness;
      No weakness has He.
    He's strong and in vigor,
      How buoyant is He!
    His Life in the glory
      My life may be;
    His Life in the glory
      My life may be.

4   There's a Man in the glory
      Whose Life is for me.
    His peace is abiding;
      How patient is He!
    He's joyful and radiant,
      Expecting to see
    His Life in the glory
      Lived out in me;
    His Life in the glory
      Lived out in me.

Composition for prophecy with main point and sub-points: _____

_____

_____

_____

_____

_____

_____

_____

_____

_____

_____

_____

_____

_____

_____

_____

_____

_____

_____

_____

_____

_____

_____

_____

_____

_____

_____

_____

_____

_____

_____

_____

_____

_____

_____

The Sign of Christ's Incarnation
and
the Unveiling of Christ as the Wonderful One

Scripture Reading: Isa. 7:11-14; 8:8; 9:6-7; 63:16; 64:8

Day 1 I. **Regarding God's economy, the intrinsic connection between the books of history in the Old Testament and their fulfillment in the New Testament is in Isaiah 7:14 and 9:6; these verses indicate that God would put humanity upon Himself, thereby mingling divinity with humanity (John 1:14; Luke 1:35; Matt. 1:18, 20).**

II. **In Isaiah 7:14 we have the sign of Christ's incarnation:**

   A. Jehovah wanted Ahaz, king of Judah, to ask for a sign (vv. 10-25); this sign is related to the ushering in of Christ, who was born of a virgin.

   B. Isaiah prophesied that the very God of Israel would become a human child born of a virgin and that His name would be called Immanuel (v. 14):

      1. The sign of a virgin conceiving and bearing a son covers the entire Bible from Genesis 11 through Revelation 22.

      2. The actual fulfillment of this sign was the birth of a son by Isaiah's wife; the ultimate fulfillment was the incarnation, in which Jesus Christ was born of the virgin Mary as a child of a dual nature, the divine nature and the human nature, issuing in Immanuel, "God with us" (Isa. 8:3; Matt. 1:23; Luke 1:35).

   C. The land of Immanuel (Isa. 8:8) is the land of Judah, the Holy Land, as the territory of Immanuel, God with us; this land, which was invaded by the army of Assyria, is the land that Christ will inherit to build up His millennial kingdom with His two elect peoples, the chosen Jews as His earthly people and the chosen believers as His heavenly people.

Day 2 D. We should consider the sign of a virgin conceiving

and bearing a son—the sign of Christ's incarnation—in relation to Satan's use of Babylon to oppose
God and God's economy (13:1, 19; 14:4, 11-15; 21:9;
47:1; 48:20):

1. In the Bible the result of Satan's work is Babylon; his opposition to God began with Babylon and will end with Babylon (Gen. 11:1-9;
   Rev. 17—18).
2. Babylon was the worst nation in offending
   God, and its king was one with Satan (Isa. 14:4,
   11-15); therefore, Babylon is God's number
   one enemy, being both the beginning and the
   conclusion of human government, and it will be
   thoroughly judged, condemned, and punished
   by God (21:9; Jer. 51:8-9; Rev. 14:8; 18:2).
3. Even the termination of Babylon is included
   in the sign of a virgin bearing a son called
   Immanuel (Isa. 7:14; 8:8).

E. The prophecy in Isaiah 7:14 concerning Immanuel can be seen in fulfillment in Matthew 1:20-23:

1. The child born of a human virgin is Emmanuel, God with man:
   a. God was begotten in the virgin Mary of the
      Holy Spirit (v. 20).
   b. The child born of Mary was a "God-man
      child"—a divine-human child.
2. God Himself came to be both God and man,
   the God-man, to be Jesus—Jehovah the
   Savior (v. 21).
3. Jesus was the name given by God, whereas
   Emmanuel was the name by which man
   called Him (v. 23):
   a. He was called by those who experienced
      Him Emmanuel—God with us.

Day 3   b. The more we experience the Lord Jesus, the
      more we will know that He is Emmanuel.

F. The practical Immanuel, the presence of the
Triune God, is the Spirit of reality (John 1:14;
14:16-20; 1 Cor. 15:45b):

1. He is with us in our gatherings and all our days (Matt. 18:20; 28:20).
2. He is with us in our spirit, which today is the land of Immanuel (2 Tim. 4:22; Isa. 8:6-8).

G. Immanuel is all-inclusive (Phil. 1:19):

1. He is first our Savior (Luke 2:11), then our Redeemer (John 1:29; Rom. 3:24), then our Life-giver (1 Cor. 15:45b), and then the all-inclusive, indwelling Spirit (John 14:16-20; Rom. 8:9-11).
2. Actually, the content of the entire New Testament is an Immanuel (Matt. 1:23; 18:20; 28:20; Rev. 21:3), and all the believers in Christ, as the members of Christ, are a part of this great Immanuel, the corporate Christ (1 Cor. 12:12; Col. 3:10-11).
3. The sign of Immanuel consummates in the New Jerusalem, which will be the aggregate of Immanuel, the totality of God being with us (Rev. 21:2-3, 10).

Day 4 **III. In Isaiah 9:6-7 we have the unveiling of Christ as the wonderful One:**

A. Christ is mentioned as a child born to us and as a Son given to us (v. 6):

1. The words *to us* indicate that this is not a doctrine but an experience.
2. The repetition of *to us* indicates a strong emphasis, showing that whatever is revealed in this verse is *to us* in a very personal, subjective, and experiential way.
3. Christ as the child, the Son, the Wonderful Counselor, the Mighty God, the Eternal Father, and the Prince of Peace is for our experience (v. 6).

B. The child born to us is both human and divine, and the Son given to us is divine:

1. The divine Son was given through the birth of the divine-human child (John 3:16):

a. The word *child* in Isaiah 9:6 implies God,

implies man, implies God becoming a man, and implies God and man mingled together as one.

  b. This child of both the divine and human natures born of a human virgin is also the Son given in the divine nature by the Eternal Father.

  c. The child born in verse 6 is the One born of a virgin and called Immanuel in 7:14.

 2. The Eternal Father gave us a gift, and that gift was His Son, who became the God-man (John 3:16; 4:10; Rom. 6:23; 1 John 5:11-12).

C. Mighty God is the name of the child, and Eternal Father—the Father in the Godhead—is the name of the Son (Isa. 63:16; 64:8; John 5:43; 10:30; 14:10, 26).

D. Isaiah 9:6 reveals clearly that the child is the Mighty God and that the Son is the Eternal Father:

 1. The Son in Isaiah 9:6 bears two main denotations:

  a. One denotation is that He is the son of a human virgin who was born of her; the other denotation is that He is also the Son of the Most High (7:14; Matt. 1:23; Luke 1:32).

  b. The Son as the son of Mary with the human nature was born, and the Son as the Son of the Most High with the divine nature was given through the birth of the son of Mary (vv. 31-33).

  c. This wonderful Son was born of the human source and given from the divine source; He is both human and divine (John 3:16; Gal. 4:4).

Day 5   2. According to Isaiah 9:6, the Son given to us is called the Eternal Father, the Father of eternity, the One who is self-existing and ever-existing:

  a. The Father in the Godhead is the Father of eternity, and according to verse 6 the Son

is also the Father of eternity, the Eternal
Father.

b. There is only one Eternal Father, the Father
who is self-existing and ever-existing.

3. Isaiah 9:6 is confirmed and strengthened by
John 14:7-11:

a. In verse 9 the Lord said, "He who has seen
Me has seen the Father."

b. The Father and the Son are one; thus, if we
confess the Son, we have the Father also
(10:30; 1 John 2:23).

4. The prophet Isaiah uses 63:16 and 64:8 as a
further development of what he prophesied
concerning Christ as the Eternal Father in
9:6:

a. In 64:8 he says that the Eternal Father is
our Creator, and in 63:16, that the Eternal
Father is our Redeemer.

b. The Eternal Father being both our Creator
and our Redeemer confirms and strengthens the understanding that the Redeemer,
Christ, is the Eternal Father, the holy
Father in the Godhead.

c. From the revelation in the entire book
of Isaiah, we can conclude that *Eternal
Father* in 9:6 refers to both Jehovah and
Jesus; hence, although He is the Son, His
name is called Eternal Father.

E. For the government to be upon Christ's shoulder
means that the divine administration is upon the
shoulder of this child who is born and this Son
who is given (v. 6).

Day 6   F. Christ is the Wonderful Counselor; our Counselor
is the Mighty God, who gives us counsel and is the
power and strength to carry out this counsel (v. 6).

G. The title *Prince of Peace* is related to government
(vv. 6-7):

1. When we have Christ as the Prince of Peace,
we have His ruling, His government, and we

enjoy His peace, which comes from His inner
ruling (Eph. 2:14-15; 4:3; Col. 3:15).

2. The government, which is upon His shoulder,
will be increased with His peace without end
(Isa. 9:7).

3. He will be upon the throne of David to rule
over His kingdom and to establish His kingdom in justice and righteousness, first in the
millennial kingdom and then in the new
heaven and new earth unto eternity (Luke
1:31-33).

IV. **In Isaiah 7:14 and 9:6-7 we have the high peak
of the divine revelation:**

A. God became man for the purpose of accomplishing His economy by making man God in life and in
nature but not in the Godhead through the processes of incarnation, human living, crucifixion,
resurrection, and ascension (John 1:1, 14, 29; 3:14;
7:39; 12:24; 20:17, 22).

B. God became man to redeem man back to Himself
and to make His redeemed people God in life and
in nature but not in the Godhead so that He might
have for eternity a universal, corporate expression of Himself (Rom. 8:3; 3:24; 1:3-4; 8:9-11, 29;
12:4-5; Rev. 1:5-6; 5:6, 10; 21:2, 10).

Definition - Intrinsic: Basic and essential belonging to something as one of the basic and essential features that make it **Morning Nourishment** *What it is.*

Isa.   Therefore the Lord Himself will give you a sign:
7:14   Behold, the virgin will conceive and will bear a son,
      and she will call his name Immanuel.
Luke   ...The Holy Spirit will come upon you, and the power of
1:35   the Most High will overshadow you; therefore also the
      holy thing which is born will be called the Son of God.

God's economy is centered in Christ with His organic Body, the church, which will consummate in the New Jerusalem. Regarding God's economy, the intrinsic connection between the books of history in the Old Testament and their fulfillment in the New Testament is in Isaiah 7:14 and 9:6. These verses indicate that God would put humanity upon Himself, mingling His divinity with humanity. Through His incarnation Christ became the God-man, a person both divine and human, having His divinity mingled with His humanity. The incarnation was, therefore, a great event in the universe. (*Life-study of 1 & 2 Kings*, p. 135)

Today's Reading

I would like to say a word concerning the relationship between the Old Testament history and the fulfillment of God's economy in the New Testament....We need to see that the prophetic books go together with the history of Israel....Isaiah 7:14 says, "Behold, the virgin will conceive and will bear a son, and she will call his name Immanuel."...This is the Triune God becoming a child. As Isaiah strengthened and helped the kings of Israel, he prophesied that the very God of Israel would become a human child born of a virgin. (*Life-study of 1 & 2 Kings*, pp. 111-112)

We will consider [the sign of Christ's incarnation given to Ahaz, king of Judah (Isa. 7:14),] in relation to Satan's use of Babylon to oppose God and God's economy. The New Testament begins with the sign of a virgin conceiving and bearing a son, whose name is called Immanuel, God with us (Matt. 1:22-23)....This great sign covers the entire Bible from Genesis 11 to Revelation 22.

Jehovah wanted Ahaz to ask for a sign (Isa. 7:10-25). This sign is related to the ushering in of Christ, who was born of a virgin....

Ahaz said that he would not ask and would not try Jehovah (v. 12). Isaiah considered this as exhausting the patience of his God (v. 13). ...Verse 14 says, "Therefore the Lord Himself will give you a sign: Behold, the virgin will conceive and will bear a son, and she will call his name Immanuel." Immanuel means "God with us." This word concerning a virgin bearing a son is quoted in Matthew 1:23 and applied to the Lord Jesus. (*Life-study of Isaiah,* pp. 51, 44)

The sign in Isaiah 7:14 has had both an actual fulfillment and a real fulfillment....The actual fulfillment was the birth of a son by Isaiah's wife. The real fulfillment of the sign given by God to Ahaz, king of Judah, was the Lord's incarnation (Matt. 1:20-23), which issued in Immanuel, that is, God with us, for the salvation of God's people. All God's people, those who are of Israel and those who are of the church, are saved by Immanuel.

The child born of a human virgin is Immanuel, God with man (Isa. 7:14; 9:6a). He was a human child born of a human virgin, yet He was also the very God. Isaiah was written about seven hundred years before Christ's incarnation, yet it speaks of a child born who would be the very God. This child was a "God-man child," a child of a dual nature, the divine nature and the human nature. He was a divine-human child.

The expression "Your land, O Immanuel" (8:8) indicates that the land of Judah, the Holy Land, is Christ's territory invaded by the conquering army of the king of Assyria. This is the land that Christ will inherit to build up His millennial kingdom with His two elect peoples, the chosen Jews and the chosen believers.

If we are those who know the Bible, we should pray for the current Middle East situation in this way: "Lord Jesus, You are Immanuel. Lord, remember the good land promised by God to His people. That is Your land. O Immanuel, the invaders are filling up Your land. How long, Lord, will You allow this to continue?" I hope that we will begin to pray in this way. (*Life-study of Isaiah,* pp. 47, 240, 46)

Further Reading: Life-study of Isaiah, msg. 7; Life-study of 1 & 2 Kings, msgs. 17, 20

Enlightenment and inspiration: _____

_____
_____

Morning Nourishment

Matt.   ...Behold, an angel of the Lord appeared to him in a
1:20-21   dream, saying, Joseph, son of David, do not be afraid
              to take Mary your wife, for that which has been
              begotten in her is of the Holy Spirit. And she will bear
              a son, and you shall call His name Jesus, for *it is* He
              who will save His people from their sins.

If we read the New Testament carefully, we will see that the
warfare between Satan and God will be ended by the fighting
between Christ with His faithful followers and Antichrist with
his followers (Rev. 17:12-15). Antichrist...will be the one who will
form an alliance with the ten toes of the image in Daniel 2 and be
their leader. In a spiritual sense, Antichrist will be a part of Babylon. The head is Babylon, and the leader of the toes is also Babylon. This indicates that the opposition to God began with Babylon
and that it will end with Babylon. When Babylon has been terminated and destroyed, the kingdom will come. This kingdom will
be composed of the two elect peoples of God, Israel and the believers. (*Life-study of Isaiah,* p. 53)

Today's Reading

We need to see clearly that the sign of a virgin conceiving and
bearing a son covers the Bible from Genesis 11 to Revelation 22.
Today we are still in the stage of the fulfillment of this sign, the
sign of a son consummating in Immanuel. As this sign continues
to be fulfilled, the war between Babylon and Jerusalem is still
raging. Today's Babylon has two sides: the spiritual, or religious,
side, which is the Roman Church, and the material side, which
will be the city of Rome.

According to the principle of the divine revelation, the first
nation used by Satan to frustrate God from accomplishing His
eternal economy was Babel in Genesis 11. *Babel* was an ancient
name for *Babylon.* At Babel rebellious people built a tower and a
city in order to make a name for themselves (Gen. 11:4). Eventually, after many centuries, Babel was enlarged to become Babylon....All the Gentile nations used by Satan against God began

from Babylon. This human opposition to God is signified by the human image in Daniel 2. This image includes Babylon (the head of gold), followed by the Medo-Persians (the breast and arms of silver), the Greeks (the belly and thighs of brass), and the Romans (the legs of iron). (*Life-study of Isaiah,* pp. 53, 52)

Babylon was the worst nation in offending God, and its king was one with Satan (Isa. 14:4, 11-15). Babylon, therefore, is God's number one enemy, being both the beginning and the conclusion of human government on earth. Babylon will be thoroughly condemned, punished, and judged by God. God will judge Babylon to such an extent that nothing of Babylon will remain in the universe. Thus, when God destroys the restored religious and political Babylon the Great, He will rid the earth of His number one enemy, which rebels against God, exalts man, and worships idols. (*Life-study of Jeremiah,* p. 253)

Even the termination of Babylon is included in the sign of a virgin conceiving a son called Immanuel.

God was begotten in the virgin Mary of the Holy Spirit....Before Jesus was born of a virgin, God was begotten in her [Matt. 1:20], born into her. That which was begotten in Mary was of the Holy Spirit. The divine essence out of the Holy Spirit had been generated in Mary's womb before she delivered the child Jesus. God was born into Mary and remained in Mary's womb for nine months. Then...Jesus, Immanuel, was delivered out of Mary's womb. First, God was begotten in the virgin Mary of the Holy Spirit. Then, a human child was brought forth with the divine nature, out of a human virgin, to be a God-man (v. 23a).

This One was named Jesus—Jehovah the Savior (v. 21). Jesus is not only a man but also Jehovah; He is Jehovah becoming our salvation, our Savior.

He was called by the ones who experienced Him Emmanuel—God with us (v. 23b). (*Life-study of Isaiah,* pp. 47, 240-241)

Further Reading: Life-study of Isaiah, msg. 8; *Life-study of Jeremiah,* msgs. 36-38

Enlightenment and inspiration: _____

_____

_____

_____

Morning Nourishment

Matt. "Behold, the virgin shall be with child and shall bear
  1:23 a son, and they shall call His name Emmanuel"
        (which is translated, God with us).
  18:20 For where there are two or three gathered into My
        name, there am I in their midst.
2 Tim. The Lord be with your spirit. Grace be with you.
  4:22

Christ is Emmanuel, God with us. "Us" refers to the saved
ones, the believers. Day by day we have Christ as Emmanuel.
Whenever we have some experience of the Lord Jesus, we shall
realize that He is God with us. God said that His name would be
called Jesus, [Jehovah the Savior]. But as we receive Him and
experience Him, we realize that Jesus is Emmanuel, God with us.

When we call on Jesus, we have the sense that God is with us. We
call on the Lord Jesus and we find God. Jesus is not only the Son of
God but also God Himself. When we call on Jesus, we have Jehovah,
we have the Savior, we have salvation, and we have God with us.

The more we experience the Lord Jesus, the more we shall
know that He is Emmanuel, God with us. As we experience Him,
we may say, "This is God! This is not God far away from me, or
God in the heavens, but God with me." In our experience Jesus
truly is Emmanuel. (*The Conclusion of the New Testament*, p. 286)

Today's Reading

According to Matthew 18:20, whenever we are gathered together
into the name of Jesus, He is with us. This is Emmanuel, God with
us. The presence of Jesus in our gatherings is actually God with us.

At the end of Matthew 28:20 the Lord says, "Behold, I am with
you all the days until the consummation of the age." Here the
Lord promises to be with us in His resurrection with all authority
all the days until the consummation of the age, that is, until the
end of this age. "All the days" includes today. The Lord Jesus as
Emmanuel is with us now, today!

Today Christ is not only among us; He is in our spirit [2 Tim.
4:22]....This One who is with our spirit is Emmanuel, God with us.

Today the Lord's presence is the Spirit. We cannot separate

the Spirit from the presence of Jesus. The Spirit is simply the reality of the Lord's presence (John 14:16-20). This presence is Emmanuel, God with us. (*The Conclusion of the New Testament,* pp. 286-287)

Immanuel is all-inclusive. He includes the Savior, the Redeemer, the Life-giver, and the all-inclusive Spirit. Immanuel is first our Savior, then our Redeemer, then our Life-giver, and then the all-inclusive, indwelling Spirit. We need to realize that the all-inclusive Spirit is Immanuel. On the one hand, this all-inclusive Spirit is the Shoot of Jehovah; on the other hand, He is the Fruit of the earth (Isa. 4:2). He is God and man. Such a one is the life-giving Spirit (1 Cor. 15:45).

In Isaiah Christ is unveiled first as the Shoot of Jehovah (4:2a) and then as the Fruit of the earth (4:2b), as a canopy to cover all the interests of God in the whole universe (4:5), and as a tabernacle overshadowing God's chosen people (4:6). Eventually, this Christ becomes the center of an all-inclusive sign—the sign of a virgin conceiving and bearing a son.

The real fulfillment of this sign was the Lord's incarnation (Matt. 1:20-23). When Christ came, He was Immanuel, which means God with us (Matt. 1:23). Christ is God with us. This is revealed not only in Matthew 1 but also in Matthew 28, where the Lord Jesus says, "Behold, I am with you all the days until the consummation of the age" (v. 20). Actually, the entire New Testament is an Immanuel, and we are now a part of this great Immanuel that will consummate in the New Jerusalem in the new heaven and new earth for eternity.

The Bible of sixty-six books consummates in the New Jerusalem (Rev. 21—22), and the New Jerusalem is the aggregate of Immanuel. The sign of Immanuel consummates in the New Jerusalem—the totality of God being with us. (*Life-study of Isaiah,* pp. 47-48, 53-54, 86)

Further Reading: Life-study of Isaiah, msg. 13; Life-study of Matthew, msgs. 5-6; The Triune God to Be Life to the Tripartite Man, ch. 9

Enlightenment and inspiration: _____

_____

_____

_____

Morning Nourishment

**Isa. For a child is born to us, a Son is given to us; and
9:6 the government is upon His shoulder; and His
name will be called Wonderful Counselor, Mighty
God, Eternal Father, Prince of Peace.**

What is revealed in Isaiah 9:6 is very personal and subjective
to us. It does not say, "A child is born, a Son is given." It says, "A Son
is given *to us.*" The phrase *to us,* especially by its repetition, indicates a strong emphasis, showing that whatever is revealed in
this verse is "to us" in a very personal, subjective and experiential
way. Not only is the "child," the "Son," for our personal experience,
but also all that His four names unfold is for our personal experience. Christ as the Wonderful Counselor, the Mighty God, and the
Prince of Peace is all for our personal experience. In this context,
the Eternal Father must also be for our personal experience. He is
our Wonderful Counselor, our Mighty God, our Prince of Peace,
and also our Eternal Father. Since the Wonderful Counselor, the
Mighty God, and the Prince of Peace are ours, the Eternal Father
must also be ours. (*Contending for the Faith: The Truth concerning the Trinity—Two Answers by Witness Lee,* pp. 24-25)

Today's Reading

In Isaiah 9:6-7 we see the unveiling of Christ as the wonderful
One.…Verse 6a says, "For a child is born to us, / A Son is given to
us." Once again, this involves the sign of a virgin conceiving and
bearing a son. In 9:6 the child born to us is both human and
divine, and the Son given to us is divine. Without the birth of the
human and divine child, there would have been no way for God to
give His divine Son to us. The divine Son was given (John 3:16)
through the birth of the human child.

The word *child* in 9:6 implies God, implies man, implies God
becoming a man, and implies God and man mingled together as
one. Such a child was a God-man. This child of both the divine and
human natures born of a human virgin was also a Son given in
the divine nature by the Eternal Father.…The child born in 9:6 is
the One born of a virgin and called Immanuel in 7:14.

The prophecy in Isaiah 9:6 concerning Christ as the wonderful One can be seen in its fulfillment in John 3:16. Isaiah 9:6 says that "a child is born to us, a Son is given to us." John 3:16 says, "For God so loved the world that He gave His only begotten Son." John 3:16 is based upon Isaiah 9:6. A Son was given by a child being born. In the birth of that child, there was a gift given by God—His Son. That child was both a man-child and a God-child, that is, a God-man child. The Eternal Father gave us a gift, and that gift was His Son, who became the God-man. (*Life-study of Isaiah*, pp. 57, 239-240, 242)

His name shall be called Wonderful Counselor and Prince of Peace. Between these names, we have Mighty God and Eternal Father. Undoubtedly, "Mighty God" is the name of the child and "Eternal Father" is the name of the Son. Therefore, according to the two lines of this verse, the child born to us is called the Mighty God and the Son given to us is called the Eternal Father. (*Contending for the Faith: The Truth concerning the Trinity—Two Answers by Witness Lee*, p. 22)

The Son in Isaiah 9:6 bears two main denotations. One is that the Son is the son of a human virgin who was born of her (Isa. 7:14; Matt. 1:23). The other denotation is that the Son is also the Son of the Most High. Gabriel told Mary in Luke 1:32 that the One conceived in her womb would be called the Son of the Most High. In this sense the Son was not to be born but to be given. This being given, though, is related to being born. The Son as the son of Mary with the human nature was born, and the Son as the Son of the Most High with the divine nature was given through the son of Mary's being born. This wonderful Son was not only born of the human source, but also given from the divine source. He is both human and divine. (*Elders' Training, Book 4: Other Crucial Matters concerning the Practice of the Lord's Recovery*, p. 16)

Further Reading: Contending for the Faith: The Truth concerning the Trinity—Two Answers by Witness Lee, pp. 19-27; *Life-study of Isaiah*, msg. 9

Enlightenment and inspiration: _____

_____

_____

_____

Morning Nourishment

Isa. For You are our Father, since Abraham does not know
63:16 us, and Israel does not acknowledge us. You, Jehovah,
are our Father; our Redeemer from eternity is Your
name.

64:8 But now, Jehovah, You are our Father; we are the
clay; and You, our Potter; and all of us are the work of
Your hand.

Isaiah 9:6 says, "For a child is born to us, / A Son is given to us
...And His name will be called...Mighty God, / Eternal Father."
According to this verse, the Son given to us is called the Eternal
Father, or the Father of eternity.

Not long ago a certain preacher said that the Father in Isaiah
9:6 is merely similar in meaning to the title "father of his country"
applied to Washington and the "father of electricity" applied to Edi-
son. Even if we accept this kind of understanding, we need to ask of
what father is the Son. According to Isaiah 9:6, He is the Father of
eternity. The title "Father of eternity" actually means "Eternal
Father." Some versions translate the Hebrew in this way. The Father
of eternity means the Father who exists forever, the eternal
Father. The phrase "of eternity" denotes One who is self-existing
and everlasting. Therefore, the Father of eternity is the Father who
is self-existing and ever-existing. (*Life-study of Exodus*, p. 1772)

Today's Reading

Who is this Father who is self-existing and ever-existing? Are
there two such Fathers—the Father in the Godhead and another
Father who is the Son in Isaiah 9:6? The answer to this question is
that the Father in the Godhead is the Father of eternity, and according to Isaiah 9:6 the Son is also the Father of eternity. There are not
two divine Fathers! There is only one Father of eternity, the Father
who is self-existing and ever-existing. (*Life-study of Exodus*, p. 1772)

In this universe there is just one divine Father. How can there
be two divine Fathers? The critics say, "The Father in Isaiah 9:6
is not the Holy Father with the Son and the Holy Spirit. This
Father is the Father of the age to come, the Father of Israel, or the

Father of something else." But do you believe that the Father in Isaiah 9:6 is separate from the unique Father of the Godhead? Nearly every truth in the Bible has more than one verse to substantiate it. Isaiah 9:6 is confirmed and strengthened by John 14:7-11, where the Lord makes it clear to the disciples that He and the Father are one. In John 10:30 He told the Jews the same thing. Who can deny that according to the pure revelation of the Bible the Son is the Father? Do not listen to the traditional talk. Others may care for their tradition, but we only care for the pure revelation according to the Bible. (*Young People's Training,* p. 80)

Isaiah 63:16 says, "You, Jehovah, are our Father;/Our Redeemer from eternity is Your name." And Isaiah 64:8 says, "Jehovah, You are our Father;/We are the clay; and You, our Potter;/And all of us are the work of Your hand." The prophet Isaiah used these two verses as a further development of what he prophesied concerning Christ as the Father of eternity in Isaiah 9:6. In 64:8 Isaiah tells us that the Father of eternity in 9:6 is our Creator, and in 63:16 he tells us that the Father of eternity is our Redeemer. In the whole Bible, Christ is revealed as our Creator and especially as our Redeemer (John 1:3; Heb. 1:10; Rom. 3:24; Titus 2:14). The Father of eternity being both our Creator and our Redeemer not only confirms but also strengthens the understanding that the Redeemer, Christ, is the Father of eternity, the holy Father in the Godhead. Hence, to say that the Eternal Father, or the Father of eternity, in Isaiah 9:6 is some kind of Father, other than the Father in the Godhead, is not according to the context of the whole book of Isaiah. (*Contending for the Faith: The Truth concerning the Trinity—Two Answers by Witness Lee,* p. 25)

Isaiah 9:6b tells us that "the government is upon His shoulder." This means that the divine administration is upon the shoulder of this child who is born and this Son who is given. (*Life-study of Isaiah,* p. 57)

Further Reading: Young People's Training, ch. 6; Elders' Training, Book 3: The Way to Carry Out the Vision, ch. 3

Enlightenment and inspiration: _____

_____

_____

_____

Morning Nourishment

Isa. To the increase of *His* government and to *His* peace
9:7 there is no end, upon the throne of David and over
His kingdom, to establish it and to uphold it in justice
and righteousness from now to eternity....

Eph. Being diligent to keep the oneness of the Spirit in the
4:3 uniting bond of peace.

Col. And let the peace of Christ arbitrate in your hearts, to
3:15 which also you were called in one Body; and be
thankful.

His name is called: "Wonderful Counselor, Mighty God, Eternal Father, Prince of Peace." According to the composition, "Wonderful Counselor" and "Mighty God" should be one pair, and "Eternal Father" and "Prince of Peace" should be another pair. This Wonderful Messiah, as the child born to the children of Israel and a Son given to them, is a Counselor, even a Wonderful Counselor to them, who gives them the wonderful counsels all the time and does everything for them. To them He is also God, even the mighty God, who is able to carry out whatever counsel He makes for them as their Counselor. In addition, He is also their Father, from eternity as their source, who fosters them and takes care of them all the time from eternity and through all the generations. He is also a Prince to them, who is their peace, gives them peace, and brings them into peace. (*Elders' Training, Book 4: Other Crucial Matters concerning the Practice of the Lord's Recovery*, pp. 16-17)

Today's Reading

He is...the Prince of Peace. This title is related to government. Isaiah 9:6 says, "The government is upon His shoulder," and verse 7 says, "To the increase of His government and to His peace there is no end." In Luke 1 the angel Gabriel said to Mary that "He will reign over the house of Jacob forever, and of His kingdom there will be no end" (v. 33).

When we have Him, we have His ruling, His government, His peace. When a husband is angry with his wife, he is not under any ruling, so there is no peace. If he would silently receive the cross and receive Christ as the Prince ruling over him, he would immediately have peace within. This peace comes from Christ's inner ruling. The government is upon the shoulder of Christ, the wonderful One (Isa. 9:6). The government which is upon His shoulder will be increased with His peace without end. He will be upon the throne of David to rule over His kingdom, to establish and uphold His kingdom in justice and righteousness firstly in the millennium and then in the new heaven and new earth unto eternity (Isa. 9:7). (*Life-study of Isaiah*, pp. 243, 244)

Isaiah 9:6 says, "For a child is born to us...And His name will be called / Wonderful Counselor, / Mighty God, / Eternal Father." This is God becoming man for the purpose of accomplishing His economy by making man God in life and in nature (but not in the Godhead). His becoming a man was for the purpose of making man God in life and in nature through the process of incarnation, human living, crucifixion, an all-inclusive death, and resurrection. In resurrection He, as the last Adam in the flesh, became a life-giving Spirit (1 Cor. 15:45b). This life-giving Spirit is the very God who became a man, lived on earth in humanity for thirty-three and a half years, died on the cross, and entered into resurrection, in which He became the life-giving Spirit.

God redeemed man for the purpose of making the redeemed man God in life and in nature so that God can have a consummation of His economy in the Body of Christ as the enlargement of Christ. This Body of Christ will consummate in the New Jerusalem as God's full expression and enlargement for eternity. In typology the history of the kings is linked to God's becoming a man to redeem man back to Himself that He might make His redeemed people God in life and in nature so that He might have for eternity a universal, corporate expression of Himself. This, in brief, is God's economy. (*Life-study of 1 & 2 Kings*, pp. 112, 122)

Further Reading: Elders' Training, Book 4: Other Crucial Matters concerning the Practice of the Lord's Recovery, ch. 1; Life-study of Isaiah, msg. 35

Enlightenment and inspiration: _____

_____

_____

Hymns, #84

1 Hark! the herald angels sing,
  "Glory to the new-born King;
 Peace on earth, and mercy mild;
  God and sinners reconciled."
 Joyful, all ye nations, rise,
  Join the triumph of the skies;
 With angelic hosts proclaim,
  "Christ is born in Bethlehem."

 (Repeat the last two lines)

2 Christ, by highest heav'n adored,
  Christ, the everlasting Lord:
 Late in time behold Him come,
  Offspring of a virgin's womb.
 Veiled in flesh the Godhead see,
  Hail th' incarnate Deity!
 Pleased as man with man to dwell,
  Jesus our Immanuel.

3 Hail the heav'n-born Prince of Peace!
  Hail the Sun of righteousness!
 Light and life to all He brings,
  Ris'n with healing in His wings:
 Mild He lays His glory by,
  Born that man no more may die;
 Born to raise the sons of earth;
  Born to give them second birth.

4 Come, Desire of nations, come!
  Fix in us Thy humble home:
 Rise, the woman's conqu'ring seed,
  Bruise in us the serpent's head;
 Adam's likeness now efface,
  Stamp Thine image in its place:
 Final Adam from above,
  Reinstate us in Thy love.

*Composition for prophecy with main point and
sub-points:* _____

_____

_____

_____

_____

_____

_____

_____

_____

_____

_____

_____

_____

_____

_____

_____

_____

_____

_____

_____

_____

_____

_____

_____

_____

_____

_____

_____

_____

_____

_____

_____

_____

_____

The Great Light

Scripture Reading: Isa. 9:1-5; 42:6; 49:6; 50:10-11; 2:5

Day 1   I. **The light in Genesis 1:3 is a type of Christ as the real light (John 1:4-5, 9):**
   A. Christ is the true light of the universe; He is the rising sun from on high, the bright morning star, and the Sun of righteousness (Luke 1:78; Rev. 22:16b; Mal. 4:2).
   B. The physical light in Genesis 1:3 is a type of Christ as the spiritual light for the new creation (2 Cor. 4:6; 5:17):
      1. Light is necessary for generating life; according to a great principle in the Bible, light is for life, and where light is, there is life (John 8:12; 1:9, 12).
      2. In Genesis light is for the old creation, but in the Gospel of John light is for the new creation; the old creation was brought into existence through physical light, whereas the new creation is brought into being through Christ as spiritual light (vv. 4-5, 9, 12; 8:12; 12:36; 2 Cor. 4:6).

  II. **The divine light is the nature of God's expression, it shines in the divine life, and it is the source of the divine truth (1 John 1:5-6; John 1:4; 8:12):**
   A. Light is God's shining, God's expression; when God is expressed, the nature of that expression is light (1 John 1:5).
   B. The divine light shines in the divine life, for light and life go together (John 1:4; 8:12; Psa. 36:9).
   C. The divine light is the source of the divine truth; when the divine light shines upon us, it becomes the truth, which is the divine reality (John 1:5, 9; 8:12, 32; 18:37).
   D. The divine light, which shines in the divine life

and issues in the divine truth, is embodied in the Lord Jesus, God incarnate (1:1, 4, 14; 8:12; 9:5; 14:6).

Day 2   III. **Christ is the great light for shining in darkness and for release from bondage (Isa. 9:1-5):**

A. As the great light, Christ is the true light, the light of life (John 1:9, 4; 8:12):

1. Christ is the unique light; apart from Him there is no light (12:46).

2. In order to have true light, we must have Christ in an experiential way (Micah 7:8; John 8:12).

3. We can see light only in the light of Christ; if we want light, we must receive Christ and touch Christ (Psa. 36:9b).

B. As the great light, Christ shines upon the people walking in darkness and upon those dwelling in the land of the shadow of death (Isa. 9:2; John 1:5; Acts 26:18; Col. 1:13):

1. Christ is the light to be the salvation of God (Isa. 49:6).

2. Christ saves us by shining on us; His shining upon us as the great light is our salvation (Acts 9:3; 22:6; 26:13).

3. The inner shining of Christ is His saving us from the darkness of death (Isa. 9:2; Matt. 1:21, 23; 4:16; 2 Cor. 4:6).

Day 3   C. Christ's shining as the great light upon God's people releases them from bondage in darkness, breaks the yoke that has been upon them, and destroys their enemies and destroys their armor (Isa. 9:3-5; 10:26-27).

D. The prophecy in Isaiah 9:2 was fulfilled in Matthew 4:16:

1. When Christ came to Galilee, the people sitting in darkness saw a great light, and to those sitting in the region and shadow of death, light sprang up.

2. Christ's ministry did not begin with earthly power but with heavenly light:

a. This light is Christ Himself as the light of

life, shining in the shadow of death (John
12:46; 8:12).

   b. Christ is the great light with the power to
attract people and capture them (Matt.
4:17-22).

  3. In particular, the Lord's teaching was the shining of a great light; every word that issued from
His mouth was an enlightening word, and
the people in darkness were enlightened by
His teaching (Mark 1:21-22).

Day 4
E. We can see the Christian life in Isaiah 9:1-5 with
the enjoyment of Christ as the great light; through
His shining, He saves us and breaks the yoke of
our burden, the staff on our shoulder, and the rod
of our oppressor.

F. Christ was called by Jehovah to be a light for the
nations (42:6):

  1. Christ is the true light that shines over the
world and enlightens every man to enliven
man for regeneration; He is the light for God's
people to receive God as life (John 1:4, 9, 12-13;
1 John 1:5; 5:11-12).

  2. Christ is the divine, marvelous light to open
the eyes of the blind and to deliver God's
chosen people out of the darkness of death,
the death-realm, the authority of Satan, into
God's life-realm of light (Isa. 42:7; Acts 26:18;
Col. 1:12-13).

  3. Although Isaiah 49:6 refers to Christ, whom
God made a light to the Gentiles so that His
salvation might reach to the ends of the earth,
the apostle Paul, who was one with Christ in
carrying out God's salvation in Christ, applied
this prophetic word to himself in his ministry
of gospel preaching (Acts 13:47).

  4. God has called us out of darkness—the expression and sphere of Satan in death—into His
marvelous light—the expression and sphere
of God in life (1 Pet. 2:9).

Day 5 **IV. We were once darkness, but we are now light in the Lord, and we should walk as children of light (Eph. 5:8-9):**

A. As God is light, so we, the children of God, are children of light (1 John 1:5; Eph. 5:8; John 12:36).

B. We are not only children of light; we are light itself because we are one with God in the Lord (Eph. 5:8; Matt. 5:14; 1 John 1:5).

C. The fruit of the light in goodness, righteousness, and truth is related to the Triune God:

1. God the Father as goodness is the nature of the fruit of the light; therefore, *goodness* in Ephesians 5:9 refers to God the Father (Matt. 19:17).

2. *Righteousness* refers to God the Son, for Christ came to accomplish God's purpose according to God's righteous procedure (Rom. 5:17-18, 21).

3. *Truth,* the expression of the fruit in the light, refers to God the Spirit, for He is the Spirit of reality (John 14:17; 16:13).

Day 6 **V. He who fears Jehovah and hears the voice of His Servant should trust in Jehovah so that he may have light while walking in darkness (Isa. 50:10-11; Psa. 139:7-12, 23-24):**

A. Those who make light for themselves and walk in their self-made light instead of God's light will suffer torment (Isa. 50:11).

B. This should be a warning to us so that we may walk in the light given by God, not in the light we make for ourselves (1 John 1:5).

C. "Come and let us walk in the light of Jehovah" (Isa. 2:5).

VI. As the shining light, the believers in Christ, the kingdom people, are like a city situated upon a mountain, a city that cannot be hidden (Matt. 5:14):

A. This light is not an individual believer; it is a corporate city built up as one entity to shine over the people surrounding it (16:18):

1. The city is the light; if there is no city, there is no light (Rev. 21:23-24).
2. If we are divided, we are finished with the shining; in order to be a shining city, we must keep the oneness and remain one entity, a corporate Body (Eph. 4:1-6; 5:8-9).
3. If we would become this city of light, we need to be built up as the Body of Christ (Matt. 16:18; Eph. 4:16):
   a. To be built up with fellow believers is the Lord's supreme and highest requirement of His faithful seekers according to the divine oneness of the Divine Trinity (John 17).
   b. Being built up with fellow partakers of the divine life is the highest virtue of one who pursues after Christ according to God's eternal economy (Eph. 2:21-22; Phil. 3:7-12).
B. Ultimately, this city of light will consummate in the holy city, the New Jerusalem, and "the nations will walk by its light" (Rev. 21:10-11, 23-24).

Morning Nourishment

John ...Jesus spoke to them, saying, <u>I am the light</u> of the
8:12 <u>world;</u> he who follows Me shall by no means walk in
       darkness, but shall have the <u>light of life.</u>
1:4 In Him was life, and the life was the light of men.

[In the Bible], the light typifies Christ as the light of the universe. The light-bearers, such as the sun and the stars, are merely
shadows, but the body is Christ. He is the true light of the universe. He is the Sun of righteousness with healing in His wings
(Mal. 4:2). He is also the bright morning star (Rev. 22:16b),
appearing privately to His lovers before the darkest hour, prior
to dawn. Furthermore, He is the great light that dispels the
death and shadow in man (Matt. 4:16). (*Truth Lessons—Level
Three*, vol. 1, p. 7)

Today's Reading

Light is necessary for generating life. According to the revelation in the Bible, light is for life. All that God created and made is
focused on life and is for life. Light and life go together. Thus, for
God's work of creation in Genesis 1, there was the need for light.
God commanded the light to come, and the light came.

The light in Genesis 1:3 is a type of Christ as the real light.
This is revealed especially in the Gospel of John. In John 1:4 and 5
we see that light is Christ, the living Word of God. When Christ
comes as the real light to shine in the darkness, the darkness cannot overcome Him. In John 8:12 the Lord says, "I am the light of
the world; he who follows Me shall by no means walk in darkness,
but shall have the light of life." In John 9:5 He goes on to say,
"While I am in the world, I am the light of the world." In Genesis
light is for the old creation, but in John 1:8 and 12 light is for the
new creation. The old creation was brought into existence
through physical light, and the new creation is brought into being
through Christ as spiritual light. The physical light in Genesis 1,
therefore, is a type of Christ as the spiritual light for God's new
creation.

Light is the nature of God's expression. Therefore, the divine light is an expressive attribute of God.

First John 1:5 says, "God is light and in Him is no darkness at all." Light is God's expression; it is God shining. When we dwell in God, who is the shining One, we are in light. The very God in whom we dwell is light. (*The Conclusion of the New Testament,* pp. 427-428, 2644)

The divine light is the essence of God's expression. When God is expressed, the essence of that expression is light. What is the divine truth? The divine truth is the issue of the divine light. When the divine light shines in us, it becomes the divine truth, which is the divine reality. This means that when the divine light shines in us, we receive the divine reality. We may also say that the divine light brings us the divine reality.

In verse 7 [John] speaks a further word concerning light: "But if we walk in the light as He is in the light, we have fellowship with one another, and the blood of Jesus His Son cleanses us from every sin." As we have indicated, the divine light is the nature, the essence, of God's expression and the source of the divine truth. This divine light shines in the divine life. Hence, if we do not have the divine life, we cannot have the divine light.

John 1:4 says, "In Him was life, and the life was the light of men." In Christ there is the divine life, and this life is the divine light. Therefore, life is light. When we have the divine life, we also have the divine light.

We have seen that the divine light is the nature of God's expression, that it is the source of the divine truth, and that it shines in the divine life. Now we must go on to see that the divine light is embodied in Jesus as God incarnate. Because He is the embodiment of the divine light, the Lord Jesus said, "I am the light of the world; he who follows Me shall by no means walk in darkness, but shall have the light of life" (John 8:12). (*Life-study of 1 John,* pp. 75-77)

Further Reading: Life-study of 1 John, msgs. 5, 7, 9; The Knowledge of Life, ch. 14

Enlightenment and inspiration: _____

_____

_____

_____

Morning Nourishment

Isa. **The people who walked in the darkness have seen a**
9:2 **great light; upon those who dwell in the land of the**
     shadow of death light has shined.
   4 **For You break the yoke of their burden and the staff**
     on their shoulder, the rod of their oppressor, as in the
     day of Midian.

Christ is the great light—the true light, the light of life (Matt. 4:12-16; John 1:9, 4). Isaiah 9:1-5, referred to in Matthew 4, unveils Christ as the great light. Then verse 6 shows that He was a child born of a human virgin and a son given by the Eternal Father. Christ as the great light shines in darkness. When we have light, everything is in order.

Isaiah also speaks of Christ as the great light for the release from bondage. The shining of the light is the release, and the darkness is the bondage. (*Life-study of Isaiah,* pp. 254, 256)

Today's Reading

Christ is the unique light. Apart from Him, there is no light. The reason so many Christians are in darkness is that they do not have Christ in an experiential way. Those in the seminaries may study theology and Christology, but they may not have the genuine experience of God and of Christ. Therefore, they are without light.

Many believers insist that the Bible is full of light....But if we do not read the Word in the Lord's presence, even our reading of the Scriptures will be in darkness. (*Life-study of Colossians,* p. 39)

Psalm 36:9b says, "In Your light we see light." We can see light only in the light of Christ. When Christ comes to us, He brings light to us that we may know ourselves thoroughly, see our true condition, and realize the corruption of our flesh. If we want light, we must receive Christ and touch Christ. Christ always brings light to us and shines on us in every way (Eph. 5:14). Therefore, Christ is the source of all lights. (*Truth Lessons—Level Three,* vol. 1, p. 7)

Christ is unveiled as the great light for the shining in darkness. He shines upon the people walking in darkness (Isa. 9:2a; John 1:5; Acts 26:18; 1 Pet. 2:9b; Col. 1:13), shining upon those dwelling in the shadow of death (Isa. 9:2b; Luke 1:78-79). Christ as the great light firstly shines. Our salvation was a shining of Christ as the great light upon us. When He shined upon us, we were saved. His shining is our salvation, and His shining is His saving of us. By His shining, darkness is gone. When darkness is gone, everything negative is gone....[Nevertheless], even though many outward negative things were dealt with, many inward negative things still remained within me. This is why we need more shining. The inner shining is Christ's saving.

The people in darkness either walk or sit. They walk in the darkness (Isa. 9:2), and they sit in the land of the shadow of death (Matt. 4:16). When a person is in darkness, he is limited to walking a little bit and sitting. Before we were saved, we were walking and sitting in darkness. Then Christ as the great light shined in the darkness and brought us into His marvelous light (1 Pet. 2:9).

We need to realize the tremendous importance of the shining of light. If the sun did not shine for one day, the entire earth would suffer. If it did not shine for three weeks, many things on the earth would die. Every day the living things of the earth live under the shining of the sun. In Luke 1:78-79, Zachariah referred to Isaiah's word when he spoke of Christ as the rising sun from on high visiting us to appear to those sitting in darkness and in the shadow of death. We Christians were the ones who were walking in darkness and sitting in the shadow of death. Then we received the Lord's shining, and that shining saved us.

Christ is also the light to be the salvation of God (Isa. 42:6b; 49:6b). Isaiah 49:6b says, "I will also set You as a light of the nations / That You may be My salvation unto the ends of the earth." Thus, God gave Christ as a light to the nations that He might be God's salvation to all the world. This light issues in Christ as the divine life to us (John 9:5; 1:4, 9; 8:12). (*Life-study of Isaiah,* pp. 255-256, 352)

Further Reading: Life-study of Isaiah, msg. 37; *The New Testament Service,* ch. 9

Enlightenment and inspiration: _____
_____
_____
_____

Morning Nourishment

John   I have come *as* a light into the world, that everyone
12:46   who believes into Me would not remain in darkness.
Matt.   And He said to them, Come after Me, and I will make
4:19-20 you fishers of men. And immediately leaving the nets,
        they followed Him.

Isaiah...speaks of Christ as the great light for the release from
bondage....Through His shining, He breaks the yoke of our burden,
the staff on our shoulder, and the rod of our oppressor. Before we
were saved, we were yoked under a heavy burden. We also had a
staff upon our shoulder, and the enemy put his rod upon us. He
yoked us, burdened us, and put us into the imprisonment of darkness. But the Lord broke the yoke of the burden of the people of God,
broke the staff on their shoulder, and broke the rod of their oppressor
as in the day of Midian when Gideon gained a great victory over the
Midianites. Later in the history of Israel, the king of Assyria came
to threaten them. He became a burden, a yoke, a staff, and a rod to
them. Isaiah described how the king of Assyria punished the children of Israel. Then Christ as the great light came to break all the
bondage by shining. (*Life-study of Isaiah,* pp. 256, 258)

Today's Reading

Isaiah 9:5 says, "For all the boots / Of those who in boots trample
in the battle-quake / And the garments / Rolled in blood / Are for
burning; / They are fuel for fire."...Christ as the great light destroys
our enemies and destroys their armor. The boots and the garments
are the enemy's armor for fighting. Christ as the great light puts
these into the fire and burns them. When the Lord Jesus fights for
us, we have the feeling that He has destroyed Satan with all of his
armor. He not only has defeated Satan but also has burned
Satan's "boots" and "garments," his armor. Satan is finished. The
boots and garments of the enemy are for burning, and they are
fuel for fire. The Lord Jesus fights against His enemy by fire.

Verse 2 says, "The people who walked in the darkness / Have
seen a great light; / Upon those who dwell in the land of the shadow
of death / Light has shined." This prophecy was fulfilled in Matthew 4.

When Christ came to Galilee, the people sitting in darkness saw a great light, and to those sitting in the region and shadow of death, light sprang up (v. 16). (*Life-study of Isaiah,* pp. 256-257, 56)

When Christ came to people, He came as a great light. Peter, Andrew, James, and John did not realize that they were in darkness as they were working by the Sea of Galilee to make a living. They did not know that they were in the shadow of death.... [Then] Christ as the great light shined upon them.

Christ's ministry did not begin with earthly power—it began with heavenly light. This light is Christ Himself as the light of life, shining in the shadow of death. When the Lord began His ministry as light, He made no display of power or authority. Rather, He walked by the seashore as a common person. But when He came to those four disciples by the Sea of Galilee, He shined upon them with a great light, shining in the darkness and in the region of the shadow of death. At that juncture, Peter, Andrew, James, and John were enlightened, attracted, and captured. Immediately they forsook their jobs and followed the Lord.

In Matthew 4 there is no record, as in Luke 5, of any miracle being done by the Lord when Peter was called. In Matthew 4 there is the great light that attracted the first disciples. This attraction did not come from what the Lord Jesus did; it came from what He was. He was a great light with the power to attract people and capture them. (*The Conclusion of the New Testament,* p. 377)

When the Lord Jesus walked through Galilee, He was a great light shining in the darkness and shining upon the people sitting in the region and shadow of death. In particular, the teaching of the Slave-Savior was the shining of a great light. Every word that issued out of His mouth was an enlightening word. Therefore, while He was teaching the people, the light was shining upon them. In this way the people in darkness were enlightened by the Lord's teaching. (*Life-study of Mark,* p. 52)

Further Reading: The Collected Works of Watchman Nee, vol. 41, pp. 17-21; vol. 37, pp. 73-81; *Life-study of Matthew,* msg. 12

Enlightenment and inspiration: _____

_____

_____

Morning Nourishment

Isa. I am Jehovah; I have called You in righteousness; I have
42:6-7 held You by the hand; I have kept You and I have given
You as a covenant for the people, as a light for the
nations; to open the eyes of the blind, to bring the prisoner out from the prison, those who dwell in darkness
from the prison house.

We can see the Christian life in Isaiah 9:1-5 with the enjoyment
of Christ as the great light, and this great light is the true light,
the light of life. The shining of the light is our salvation. Christ
saves us by shining in us. If two people are roommates, they are
prone to arguing and disagreeing with each other and bothering
each other. What can stop this…? Christ as the light can stop this.
This is why we need a morning revival with the Lord. We may dis-
agree with someone in the evening, but in the morning when we
are in the Word and in the Lord, the Lord takes the opportunity to
shine into us. There may be only a "narrow crack" in our being as
an opening to Him, but He shines into us through that opening.
Because of His shining, we are enlightened, and we may say with
tears, "Lord, forgive me." This is an example of Christ's saving us
by His shining. (Life-study of Isaiah, p. 258)

Today's Reading

In addition to our time of morning revival, we need to walk in
Christ as the light. Just as we wash our hands many times a day,
we need the washing of His blood through the confessing of our
sins under the shining of His light many times a day. This contin-
ual shining and washing is our salvation. This salvation releases
us from all bondage. Then we will be the proper harvesters and
fighters for the multiplication of the people of God, and we will
have joy, rejoicing, and gladness. Wherever Christ is preached,
there is light, shining, and salvation. There is also the breaking of
the yoke of the burden of the people of God, of the staff on their
shoulder, and of the rod of their oppressor. This is all due to Christ
being the great light.

Christ has been called by Jehovah, and He is held by His hand

and kept by Him (Isa. 42:6). This means that Christ and the God who calls are one. First, Christ has been called by Jehovah, and then Christ is held and kept by Jehovah. Therefore, Christ and God are one. This Christ has been called to be a covenant for the people (49:8b; Heb. 7:22). Christ has also been called to be a light for the nations (Isa. 49:6b; Matt. 4:13-16), to open the eyes of the blind (Isa. 42:7a; Luke 4:18; John 9:14), and to bring the prisoner out of prison and those who dwell in darkness from the prison house (Isa. 42:7b).

Christ's commission is also to be a light to the nations (42:6e; 49:6c). He is the light of life, the true light, to shine over the world and enlighten every man (John 1:4, 9; 8:12; 9:5). This light is the light of life to enliven man for regeneration (1 Pet. 1:23). He is the divine, marvelous light to deliver God's chosen people out of the darkness of death, the death-realm, the authority of Satan, into God's life-realm of light (1 Pet. 2:9b; Acts 26:18a). (*Life-study of Isaiah,* pp. 258-259, 148, 339)

[In Acts 13:47 Paul quotes Isaiah 49:6]: "I have set you as a light of the Gentiles, that you would be for salvation unto the uttermost part of the earth." This...refers to Christ as God's Servant, whom God makes a light to the Gentiles so that His salvation may reach to the end of the earth. The apostle Paul, because he was one with Christ in carrying out God's salvation in Christ, applied this prophetic word to himself in his ministry of gospel preaching for the turning of the gospel from the Jews, because of their rejection, to the Gentiles. In His ministry on earth the Lord expressed the same thing to the stubborn Jews in Luke 4:24-27. (*Life-study of Acts,* pp. 328-329)

In 1 Peter 2:9 we are told that God has called us out of darkness into His marvelous light. Darkness is the expression and sphere of Satan in death; light is the expression and sphere of God in life. God has called us, delivered us, out of Satan's death-realm of darkness into His life-realm of light (Acts 26:18; Col. 1:13). (*The Conclusion of the New Testament,* p. 198)

Further Reading: Life-study of Isaiah, msgs. 22, 46-47

Enlightenment and inspiration: _____

_____

_____

Morning Nourishment

Eph. **For you were once darkness but are now light in**
5:8-9 **the Lord; walk as children of light (for the fruit of**
the light *consists* **in all goodness and righteous-**
ness and truth).

In Ephesians 5:8 Paul says, "For you were once darkness but
are now light in the Lord; walk as children of light." We were
once not only dark, but darkness itself. Now we are not only the
children of light, but light itself (Matt. 5:14). As light is God, so
darkness is the devil. We were darkness because we were one
with the devil. Now we are light because we are one with God in
the Lord.

In this verse Paul exhorts us to "walk as children of light." As
God is light, so we, the children of God, are also the children of
light. Because we are now light in the Lord, we should walk as
children of light. (*Life-study of Ephesians,* p. 425)

Today's Reading

It is rather difficult to point out the difference between truth
and light. In our experience we may often realize God as truth to
us, as our reality. But sometimes when we get into God's presence, we sense that we are in the light. At such times, we are not
only experiencing reality, but we are in the very light itself.
Thus, the experience of light is deeper than the experience of
truth.

After commanding us to walk as children of light [Eph. 5:8],
Paul inserts in verse 9 a parenthetical statement regarding the
fruit of the light, saying that "the fruit of the light consists in all
goodness and righteousness and truth." Goodness is the nature
of the fruit of the light; righteousness is the way or the procedure
to produce the fruit of the light; and the truth is the reality, the
real expression of the fruit of the light. This expression is God
Himself. The fruit of the light must be good in nature, righteous
in procedure, and real in expression so that God may be expressed as the reality of our daily walk.

It is significant that in speaking of the fruit of the light Paul mentions only three things: goodness, righteousness, and truth. He does not speak of holiness, kindness, or humility. The reason he mentions just three things is that the fruit of the light in goodness, righteousness, and truth is related to the Triune God. Goodness refers to the nature of the fruit of light. The Lord Jesus once indicated that the only One who is good is God Himself (Matt. 19:17). Hence, goodness here denotes God the Father. God the Father as goodness is the nature of the fruit of the light.

Notice that here Paul speaks not of the work of the light nor of the conduct of the light, but of the fruit of the light. Fruit is a matter of life with its nature. The nature of the fruit of the light is God the Father.

We have pointed out that the righteousness denotes the way or the procedure of the fruit of the light. Righteousness is the procedure by which the fruit of the light is produced. In the Godhead, the Son, Christ, is our righteousness. He came to earth to produce certain things according to God's procedure, which is always righteous. Righteousness is God's way, God's procedure. Christ came to accomplish God's purpose according to His righteous procedure. Therefore, the second aspect of the fruit of the light refers to God the Son.

The truth is the expression of the fruit of the light. This fruit must be real; that is, it must be the expression of God, the shining of the hidden light. No doubt, this truth refers to the Spirit of reality, the third of the Triune God. Therefore, the Father as the goodness, the Son as the righteousness, and the Spirit as the truth, the reality, are all related to the fruit of the light.

Ephesians 5:9 is the definition of walking as children of light. If we walk as the children of light, we shall bear the fruit described in verse 9. The fruit we bear by walking as the children of the light must be in goodness, in righteousness, and in truth. The proof that we are walking as children of light is seen in the bearing of such fruit. (*Life-study of Ephesians*, pp. 426-428)

Further Reading: Life-study of Ephesians, msgs. 10, 49-50

Enlightenment and inspiration: _____

_____
_____
_____

Morning Nourishment

Matt.   You are the light of the world. It is impossible for a city
5:14   situated upon a mountain to be hidden.
Rev.   And the city has no need of the sun or of the moon
21:23-24   that they should shine in it, for the glory of God illumined it, and its lamp is the Lamb. And the nations
will walk by its light...

In Isaiah 50:10 and 11 we are told how he who fears Jehovah
and hears the voice of His servant has light while walking in
darkness. Concerning such a one, verse 10b says, "Let him trust
in the name of Jehovah, / And rely on his God." Verse 11 goes on to
give a warning about self-made light. "Indeed, all of you who kin-
dle a fire, / Who surround yourselves with firebrands, / Walk into
the light of your fire / And into the firebrands which you have lit. /
You will have this from My hand: / You will lie down in torment."
Those who make light for themselves and walk in their self-made
light instead of God's light will suffer torment. This should be a
warning to us that we may walk in the light given by God, not in
the light we make for ourselves. (*Life-study of Isaiah,* p. 174)

Today's Reading

As the shining light, the kingdom people are like a city situated upon a mountain. Such a city cannot be hidden. This is ultimately consummated in the holy city of the New Jerusalem (Rev.
21:10-11, 23-24). For many years...I could not understand how
light could be illustrated by a builded city. After I was in the practical building of the church, I saw that only by being built together
can the kingdom people be a city situated on a mountain. This city
becomes a shining light.

In Matthew 5—7 the Lord Jesus did not use the term "church."
However, the term "kingdom," used many times in these chapters, actually refers to the church....Many Christians understand
these chapters in an individualistic way. Most have not seen that
this constitution is not for individuals, but for a corporate people.
We know that this decree is for a corporate people, because the
light is not an individual person, but a builded city. This indicates

that the kingdom people need the building. If the saints in the church in your locality are not built up, but are scattered, divided, and separated, there is no city there. And as long as there is no city, there is no light, because the light is the city; the light is not an individual believer. The light is a corporate city built up as one entity to shine over the people surrounding it....Every local church in the Lord's recovery must be a builded city.

In the book of Revelation the churches are golden lampstands (Rev. 1:20). The principle of the city and the lampstand is the same: neither is individual. Both are corporate. The lampstand, like the city, is not an individual believer, but the church. If you are outside the church, you are not a part of the lampstand. In order to be part of the lampstand, you must be built into the local church. The local church, which is the lampstand, is likened by the Lord to a builded city set on the top of a mountain. If we are built up in our locality, we shall be on the mountaintop....In every locality there must be just one lampstand, one city situated on a mountain. For this, we must keep the unity and remain one entity, a corporate Body. Then we shall be able to shine....When we have truly been built together, we shall be the city on a mountaintop shining upon those around us. (*Life-study of Matthew*, pp. 204-205)

To be built up with the fellow believers is the Lord's supreme and highest requirement to His faithful seekers according to one of the divine attributes of the Divine Trinity (John 17). Our oneness, to which we testify in the Lord's table meeting, is according to the divine oneness, which is an attribute of the Divine Trinity.

Being built up with the fellow partakers of the divine life is the highest virtue of the one who pursues after Christ in God's eternal economy. Building is the highest requirement, and being built up is the highest virtue. (*The Secret of God's Organic Salvation—"The Spirit Himself with Our Spirit,"* p. 51)

Further Reading: Life-study of Matthew, msg. 16; *The Conclusion of the New Testament*, msg. 436; *The Collected Works of Watchman Nee*, vol. 44, pp. 871-873, 902-903; vol. 9, pp. 226-238

Enlightenment and inspiration: _____

_____

_____

_____

Hymns, #1259

1   See the local churches,
'Midst the earth's dark night;
Jesus' testimony,
Bearing Him as light.
Formed by Him, unmeasured,
In the Spirit's mold—
All are one in nature,
One pure work of gold.

> See the local churches,
> 'Midst the earth's dark night;
> Burning in the Spirit,
> Shining forth with Christ.

2   God in Christ, embodied,
As God's lampstand, He
Has become the Spirit,
The reality.
Spirit as the lampstand
Has been multiplied;
Many local churches,
Now are realized!

3   Caring for the churches
Is the Son of Man:
Voice of many waters,
Stars in His right hand;
Eyes aflame; His face is
Shining as the sun;
Churches—fear no trial,
He's the living One!

4   What can quench the lampstands?
Who can them defy?
More the opposition—
More they multiply!
Deeper darkness 'round them,
Brighter do they shine.
They are constituted
With the life divine.

5   Soon the local churches
Shall the Bride become,
Bringing in that city—
New Jerusalem.

Then the many lampstands
Shall one lampstand be;
Triune God expressing,
Universally.

Lo, from heav'n descending,
All the earth shall see
God's complete expression,
For eternity.

Composition for prophecy with main point and sub-points: Luke 11:33-36 Warning Not to remain in darkness Matt 6:22-24 ; Matt 20:15 ; Mark 7:22 evil eye is a wicked eye. A Semitic expression referring to the eye that entends to do evil and, by extension, to hostility, jealousy or envy

Matt 25-34 ; Luke 11:37-

Reading Schedule for the Recovery Version of the Old Testament with Footnotes

Wk.	Lord's Day	Monday	Tuesday	Wednesday	Thursday	Friday	Saturday
1	Gen 1:1-5	1:6-23	1:24-31	2:1-9	2:10-25	3:1-13	3:14-24
2	4:1-26	5:1-32	6:1-22	7:1—8:3	8:4-22	9:1-29	10:1-32
3	11:1-32	12:1-20	13:1-18	14:1-24	15:1-21	16:1-16	17:1-27
4	18:1-33	19:1-38	20:1-18	21:1-34	22:1-24	23:1—24:27	24:28-67
5	25:1-34	26:1-35	27:1-46	28:1-22	29:1-35	30:1-43	31:1-55
6	32:1-32	33:1—34:31	35:1-29	36:1-43	37:1-36	38:1—39:23	40:1—41:13
7	41:14-57	42:1-38	43:1-34	44:1-34	45:1-28	46:1-34	47:1-31
8	48:1-22	49:1-15	49:16-33	50:1-26	Exo 1:1-22	2:1-25	3:1-22
9	4:1-31	5:1-23	6:1-30	7:1-25	8:1-32	9:1-35	10:1-29
10	11:1-10	12:1-14	12:15-36	12:37-51	13:1-22	14:1-31	15:1-27
11	16:1-36	17:1-16	18:1-27	19:1-25	20:1-26	21:1-36	22:1-31
12	23:1-33	24:1-18	25:1-22	25:23-40	26:1-14	26:15-37	27:1-21
13	28:1-21	28:22-43	29:1-21	29:22-46	30:1-10	30:11-38	31:1-17
14	31:18—32:35	33:1-23	34:1-35	35:1-35	36:1-38	37:1-29	38:1-31
15	39:1-43	40:1-38	Lev 1:1-17	2:1-16	3:1-17	4:1-35	5:1-19
16	6:1-30	7:1-38	8:1-36	9:1-24	10:1-20	11:1-47	12:1-8
17	13:1-28	13:29-59	14:1-18	14:19-32	14:33-57	15:1-33	16:1-17
18	16:18-34	17:1-16	18:1-30	19:1-37	20:1-27	21:1-24	22:1-33
19	23:1-22	23:23-44	24:1-23	25:1-23	25:24-55	26:1-24	26:25-46
20	27:1-34	Num 1:1-54	2:1-34	3:1-51	4:1-49	5:1-31	6:1-27
21	7:1-41	7:42-88	7:89—8:26	9:1-23	10:1-36	11:1-35	12:1—13:33
22	14:1-45	15:1-41	16:1-50	17:1—18:7	18:8-32	19:1-22	20:1-29
23	21:1-35	22:1-41	23:1-30	24:1-25	25:1-18	26:1-65	27:1-23
24	28:1-31	29:1-40	30:1—31:24	31:25-54	32:1-42	33:1-56	34:1-29
25	35:1-34	36:1-13	Deut 1:1-46	2:1-37	3:1-29	4:1-49	5:1-33
26	6:1—7:26	8:1-20	9:1-29	10:1-22	11:1-32	12:1-32	12:1…

Reading Schedule for the Recovery Version of the Old Testament with Footnotes

Wk.	Lord's Day	Monday	Tuesday	Wednesday	Thursday	Friday	Saturday
27	☐ 14:22—15:23	☐ 16:1-22	☐ 17:1—18:8	☐ 18:9—19:21	☐ 20:1—21:17	☐ 21:18—22:30	☐ 23:1-25
28	☐ 24:1-22	☐ 25:1-19	☐ 26:1-19	☐ 27:1-26	☐ 28:1-68	☐ 29:1-29	☐ 30:1—31:29
29	☐ 31:30—32:52	☐ 33:1-29	☐ 34:1-12	☐ Josh 1:1-18	☐ 2:1-24	☐ 3:1-17	☐ 4:1-24
30	☐ 5:1-15	☐ 6:1-27	☐ 7:1-26	☐ 8:1-35	☐ 9:1-27	☐ 10:1-43	☐ 11:1—12:24
31	☐ 13:1-33	☐ 14:1—15:63	☐ 16:1—18:28	☐ 19:1-51	☐ 20:1—21:45	☐ 22:1-34	☐ 23:1—24:33
32	☐ Judg 1:1-36	☐ 2:1-23	☐ 3:1-31	☐ 4:1-24	☐ 5:1-31	☐ 6:1-40	☐ 7:1-25
33	☐ 8:1-35	☐ 9:1-57	☐ 10:1—11:40	☐ 12:1—13:25	☐ 14:1—15:20	☐ 16:1-31	☐ 17:1—18:31
34	☐ 19:1-30	☐ 20:1-48	☐ 21:1-25	☐ Ruth 1:1-22	☐ 2:1-23	☐ 3:1-18	☐ 4:1-22
35	☐ 1 Sam 1:1-28	☐ 2:1-36	☐ 3:1—4:22	☐ 5:1—6:21	☐ 7:1—8:22	☐ 9:1-27	☐ 10:1—11:15
36	☐ 12:1—13:23	☐ 14:1-52	☐ 15:1-35	☐ 16:1-23	☐ 17:1-58	☐ 18:1-30	☐ 19:1-24
37	☐ 20:1-42	☐ 21:1—22:23	☐ 23:1—24:22	☐ 25:1-44	☐ 26:1-25	☐ 27:1—28:25	☐ 29:1—30:31
38	☐ 31:1-13	☐ 2 Sam 1:1-27	☐ 2:1-32	☐ 3:1-39	☐ 4:1—5:25	☐ 6:1-23	☐ 7:1-29
39	☐ 8:1—9:13	☐ 10:1—11:27	☐ 12:1-31	☐ 13:1-39	☐ 14:1-33	☐ 15:1—16:23	☐ 17:1—18:33
40	☐ 19:1-43	☐ 20:1—21:22	☐ 22:1-51	☐ 23:1-39	☐ 24:1-25	☐ 1 Kings 1:1-19	☐ 1:20-53
41	☐ 2:1-46	☐ 3:1-28	☐ 4:1-34	☐ 5:1—6:38	☐ 7:1-22	☐ 7:23-51	☐ 8:1-36
42	☐ 8:37-66	☐ 9:1-28	☐ 10:1-29	☐ 11:1-43	☐ 12:1-33	☐ 13:1-34	☐ 14:1-31
43	☐ 15:1-34	☐ 16:1—17:24	☐ 18:1-46	☐ 19:1-21	☐ 20:1-43	☐ 21:1—22:53	☐ 2 Kings 1:1-18
44	☐ 2:1—3:27	☐ 4:1-44	☐ 5:1—6:33	☐ 7:1-20	☐ 8:1-29	☐ 9:1-37	☐ 10:1-36
45	☐ 11:1—12:21	☐ 13:1-14:29	☐ 15:1-38	☐ 16:1-20	☐ 17:1-41	☐ 18:1-37	☐ 19:1-37
46	☐ 20:1—21:26	☐ 22:1-20	☐ 23:1-37	☐ 24:1—25:30	☐ 1 Chron 1:1-54	☐ 2:1—3:24	☐ 4:1—5:26
47	☐ 6:1-81	☐ 7:1-40	☐ 8:1-40	☐ 9:1-44	☐ 10:1—11:47	☐ 12:1-40	☐ 13:1—14:17
48	☐ 15:1—16:43	☐ 17:1-27	☐ 18:1—19:19	☐ 20:1—21:30	☐ 22:1—23:32	☐ 24:1—25:31	☐ 26:1-32
49	☐ 27:1-34	☐ 28:1—29:30	☐ 2 Chron 1:1-17	☐ 2:1—3:17	☐ 4:1—5:14	☐ 6:1-42	☐ 7:1—8:18
50	☐ 9:1—10:19	☐ 11:1—12:16	☐ 13:1—15:19	☐ 16:1—17:19	☐ 18:1—19:11	☐ 20:1-37	☐ 21:1—22:12
51	☐ 23:1—24:27	☐ 25:1—26:23	☐ 27:1—28:27	☐ 29:1-36	☐ 30:1—31:21	☐ 32:1-33	☐ 33:1—34:33
52	☐ 35:1—36:23	☐ Ezra 1:1-11	☐ 2:1-70	☐ 3:1—4:24	☐ 5:1—6:22	☐ 7:1-28	☐ 8:1-36

Reading Schedule for the Recovery Version of the Old Testament with Footnotes

Wk.	Lord's Day	Monday	Tuesday	Wednesday	Thursday	Friday	Saturday
53	☐ 9:1—10:44	☐ Neh 1:1-11	☐ 2:1—3:32	☐ 4:1—5:19	☐ 6:1-19	☐ 7:1-73	☐ 8:1-18
54	☐ 9:1-20	☐ 9:21-38	☐ 10:1—11:36	☐ 12:1-47	☐ 13:1-31	☐ Esth 1:1-22	☐ 2:1—3:15
55	☐ 4:1—5:14	☐ 6:1—7:10	☐ 8:1-17	☐ 9:1—10:3	☐ Job 1:1-22	☐ 2:1—3:26	☐ 4:1—5:27
56	☐ 6:1—7:21	☐ 8:1—9:35	☐ 10:1—11:20	☐ 12:1—13:28	☐ 14:1—15:35	☐ 16:1—17:16	☐ 18:1—19:29
57	☐ 20:1—21:34	☐ 22:1—23:17	☐ 24:1—25:6	☐ 26:1—27:23	☐ 28:1—29:25	☐ 30:1—31:40	☐ 32:1—33:33
58	☐ 34:1—35:16	☐ 36:1-33	☐ 37:1-24	☐ 38:1-41	☐ 39:1-30	☐ 40:1-24	☐ 41:1-34
59	☐ 42:1-17	☐ Psa 1:1-6	☐ 2:1—3:8	☐ 4:1—6:10	☐ 7:1—8:9	☐ 9:1—10:18	☐ 11:1—15:5
60	☐ 16:1—17:15	☐ 18:1-50	☐ 19:1—21:13	☐ 22:1-31	☐ 23:1—24:10	☐ 25:1—27:14	☐ 28:1—30:12
61	☐ 31:1—32:11	☐ 33:1—34:22	☐ 35:1—36:12	☐ 37:1-40	☐ 38:1—39:13	☐ 40:1—41:13	☐ 42:1—43:5
62	☐ 44:1-26	☐ 45:1-17	☐ 46:1—48:14	☐ 49:1—50:23	☐ 51:1—52:9	☐ 53:1—55:23	☐ 56:1—58:11
63	☐ 59:1—61:8	☐ 62:1—64:10	☐ 65:1—67:7	☐ 68:1-35	☐ 69:1—70:5	☐ 71:1—72:20	☐ 73:1—74:23
64	☐ 75:1—77:20	☐ 78:1-72	☐ 79:1—81:16	☐ 82:1—84:12	☐ 85:1—87:7	☐ 88:1—89:52	☐ 90:1—91:16
65	☐ 92:1—94:23	☐ 95:1—97:12	☐ 98:1—101:8	☐ 102:1—103:22	☐ 104:1—105:45	☐ 106:1-48	☐ 107:1-43
66	☐ 108:1—109:31	☐ 110:1—112:10	☐ 113:1—115:18	☐ 116:1—118:29	☐ 119:1-32	☐ 119:33-72	☐ 119:73-120
67	☐ 119:121-176	☐ 120:1—124:8	☐ 125:1—128:6	☐ 129:1—132:18	☐ 133:1—135:21	☐ 136:1—138:8	☐ 139:1—140:13
68	☐ 141:1—144:15	☐ 145:1—147:20	☐ 148:1—150:6	☐ Prov 1:1-33	☐ 2:1—3:35	☐ 4:1—5:23	☐ 6:1-35
69	☐ 7:1—8:36	☐ 9:1—10:32	☐ 11:1—12:28	☐ 13:1—14:35	☐ 15:1-33	☐ 16:1-33	☐ 17:1-28
70	☐ 18:1-24	☐ 19:1—20:30	☐ 21:1—22:29	☐ 23:1-35	☐ 24:1—25:28	☐ 26:1—27:27	☐ 28:1—29:27
71	☐ 30:1-33	☐ 31:1-31	☐ Eccl 1:1-18	☐ 2:1—3:22	☐ 4:1—5:20	☐ 6:1—7:29	☐ 8:1—9:18
72	☐ 10:1—11:10	☐ 12:1-14	☐ S.S 1:1-8	☐ 1:9-17	☐ 2:1-17	☐ 3:1-11	☐ 4:1-8
73	☐ 4:9-16	☐ 5:1-16	☐ 6:1-13	☐ 7:1-13	☐ 8:1-14	☐ Isa 1:1-11	☐ 1:12-31
74	☐ 2:1-22	☐ 3:1-26	☐ 4:1-6	☐ 5:1-30	☐ 6:1-13	☐ 7:1-25	☐ 8:1-22
75	☐ 9:1-21	☐ 10:1-34	☐ 11:1—12:6	☐ 13:1-22	☐ 14:1-14	☐ 14:15-32	☐ 15:1—16:14
76	☐ 17:1—18:7	☐ 19:1-25	☐ 20:1—21:17	☐ 22:1-25	☐ 23:1-18	☐ 24:1-23	☐ 25:1-12
77	☐ 26:1—:21	☐ 27:1-13	☐ 28:1-29	☐ 29:1-24	☐ 30:1-33	☐ 31:1—32:20	☐ 33:1-24
78	☐ 34:1-17	☐ 35:1-10	☐ 36:1-22	☐ 37:1-38	☐ 38:1—39:8	☐ 40:1-31	

Reading Schedule for the Recovery Version of the Old Testament with Footnotes

Wk.	Lord's Day	Monday	Tuesday	Wednesday	Thursday	Friday	Saturday
79	42:1-25	43:1-28	44:1-28	45:1-25	46:1-13	47:1-15	48:1-22
80	49:1-13	49:14-26	50:1—51:23	52:1-15	53:1-12	54:1-17	55:1-13
81	56:1-12	57:1-21	58:1-14	59:1-21	60:1-22	61:1-11	62:1-12
82	63:1-19	64:1-12	65:1-25	66:1-24	Jer 1:1-19	2:1-19	2:20-37
83	3:1-25	4:1-31	5:1-31	6:1-30	7:1-34	8:1-22	9:1-26
84	10:1-25	11:1—12:17	13:1-27	14:1-22	15:1-21	16:1—17:27	18:1-23
85	19:1—20:18	21:1—22:30	23:1-40	24:1—25:38	26:1—27:22	28:1—29:32	30:1-24
86	31:1-23	31:24-40	32:1-44	33:1-26	34:1-22	35:1-19	36:1-32
87	37:1-21	38:1-28	39:1—40:16	41:1—42:22	43:1—44:30	45:1—46:28	47:1—48:16
88	48:17-47	49:1-22	49:23-39	50:1-27	50:28-46	51:1-27	51:28-64
89	52:1-34	Lam 1:1-22	2:1-22	3:1-39	3:40-66	4:1-22	5:1-22
90	Ezek 1:1-14	1:15-28	2:1—3:27	4:1—5:17	6:1—7:27	8:1—9:11	10:1—11:25
91	12:1—13:23	14:1—15:8	16:1-63	17:1—18:32	19:1-14	20:1-49	21:1-32
92	22:1-31	23:1-49	24:1-27	25:1—26:21	27:1-36	28:1-26	29:1—30:26
93	31:1—32:32	33:1-33	34:1-31	35:1—36:21	36:22-38	37:1-28	38:1—39:29
94	40:1-27	40:28-49	41:1-26	42:1—43:27	44:1-31	45:1-25	46:1-24
95	47:1-23	48:1-35	Dan 1:1-21	2:1-30	2:31-49	3:1-30	4:1-37
96	5:1-31	6:1-28	7:1-12	7:13-28	8:1-27	9:1-27	10:1-21
97	11:1-22	11:23-45	12:1-13	Hosea 1:1-11	2:1-23	3:1—4:19	5:1-15
98	6:1-11	7:1-16	8:1-14	9:1-17	10:1-15	11:1-12	12:1-14
99	13:1—14:9	Joel 1:1-20	2:1-16	2:17-32	3:1-21	Amos 1:1-15	2:1-16
100	3:1-15	4:1—5:27	6:1—7:17	8:1—9:15	Obad 1-21	Jonah 1:1-17	2:1—4:11
101	Micah 1:1-16	2:1—3:12	4:1—5:15	6:1—7:20	Nahum 1:1-15	2:1—3:19	Hab 1:1-17
102	2:1-20	3:1-19	Zeph 1:1-18	2:1-15	3:1-20	Hag 1:1-15	2:1-23
103	Zech 1:1-21	2:1-13	3:1-10	4:1-14	5:1—6:15	7:1—8:23	9:1-17
104	10:1—11:17	12:1—13:9	14:1-21	Mal 1:1-14	2:1-17	3:1-18	4:1-6

Reading Schedule for the Recovery Version of the New Testament with Footnotes

Wk.	Lord's Day	Monday	Tuesday	Wednesday	Thursday	Friday	Saturday
1	☐ Matt 1:1-2	☐ 1:3-7	☐ 1:8-17	☐ 1:18-25	☐ 2:1-23	☐ 3:1-6	☐ 3:7-17
2	☐ 4:1-11	☐ 4:12-25	☐ 5:1-4	☐ 5:5-12	☐ 5:13-20	☐ 5:21-26	☐ 5:27-48
3	☐ 6:1-8	☐ 6:9-18	☐ 6:19-34	☐ 7:1-12	☐ 7:13-29	☐ 8:1-13	☐ 8:14-22
4	☐ 8:23-34	☐ 9:1-13	☐ 9:14-17	☐ 9:18-34	☐ 9:35—10:5	☐ 10:6-25	☐ 10:26-42
5	☐ 11:1-15	☐ 11:16-30	☐ 12:1-14	☐ 12:15-32	☐ 12:33-42	☐ 12:43—13:2	☐ 13:3-12
6	☐ 13:13-30	☐ 13:31-43	☐ 13:44-58	☐ 14:1-13	☐ 14:14-21	☐ 14:22-36	☐ 15:1-20
7	☐ 15:21-31	☐ 15:32-39	☐ 16:1-12	☐ 16:13-20	☐ 16:21-28	☐ 17:1-13	☐ 17:14-27
8	☐ 18:1-14	☐ 18:15-22	☐ 18:23-35	☐ 19:1-15	☐ 19:16-30	☐ 20:1-16	☐ 20:17-34
9	☐ 21:1-11	☐ 21:12-22	☐ 21:23-32	☐ 21:33-46	☐ 22:1-22	☐ 22:23-33	☐ 22:34-46
10	☐ 23:1-12	☐ 23:13-39	☐ 24:1-14	☐ 24:15-31	☐ 24:32-51	☐ 25:1-13	☐ 25:14-30
11	☐ 25:31-46	☐ 26:1-16	☐ 26:17-35	☐ 26:36-46	☐ 26:47-64	☐ 26:65-75	☐ 27:1-26
12	☐ 27:27-44	☐ 27:45-56	☐ 27:57—28:15	☐ 28:16-20	☐ Mark 1:1	☐ 1:2-6	☐ 1:7-13
13	☐ 1:14-28	☐ 1:29-45	☐ 2:1-12	☐ 2:13-28	☐ 3:1-19	☐ 3:20-35	☐ 4:1-25
14	☐ 4:26-41	☐ 5:1-20	☐ 5:21-43	☐ 6:1-29	☐ 6:30-56	☐ 7:1-23	☐ 7:24-37
15	☐ 8:1-26	☐ 8:27—9:1	☐ 9:2-29	☐ 9:30-50	☐ 10:1-16	☐ 10:17-34	☐ 10:35-52
16	☐ 11:1-16	☐ 11:17-33	☐ 12:1-27	☐ 12:28-44	☐ 13:1-13	☐ 13:14-37	☐ 14:1-26
17	☐ 14:27-52	☐ 14:53-72	☐ 15:1-15	☐ 15:16-47	☐ 16:1-8	☐ 16:9-20	☐ Luke 1:1-4
18	☐ 1:5-25	☐ 1:26-46	☐ 1:47-56	☐ 1:57-80	☐ 2:1-8	☐ 2:9-20	☐ 2:21-39
19	☐ 2:40-52	☐ 3:1-20	☐ 3:21-38	☐ 4:1-13	☐ 4:14-30	☐ 4:31-44	☐ 5:1-26
20	☐ 5:27—6:16	☐ 6:17-38	☐ 6:39-49	☐ 7:1-17	☐ 7:18-23	☐ 7:24-35	☐ 7:36-50
21	☐ 8:1-15	☐ 8:16-25	☐ 8:26-39	☐ 8:40-56	☐ 9:1-17	☐ 9:18-26	☐ 9:27-36
22	☐ 9:37-50	☐ 9:51-62	☐ 10:1-11	☐ 10:12-24	☐ 10:25-37	☐ 10:38-42	☐ 11:1-13
23	☐ 11:14-26	☐ 11:27-36	☐ 11:37-54	☐ 12:1-12	☐ 12:13-21	☐ 12:22-34	☐ 12:35-48
24	☐ 12:49-59	☐ 13:1-9	☐ 13:10-17	☐ 13:18-30	☐ 13:31—14:6	☐ 14:7-14	☐ 14:15-24
25	☐ 14:25-35	☐ 15:1-10	☐ 15:11-21	☐ 15:22-32	☐ 16:1-13	☐ 16:14-22	☐ 16:23-31
26	☐ 17:1-19	☐ 17:20-37	☐ 18:1-14	☐ 18:15-30	☐ 18:31-43	☐ 19:1-10	☐ 19:11-27

Reading Schedule for the Recovery Version of the New Testament with Footnotes

Wk.	Lord's Day	Monday	Tuesday	Wednesday	Thursday	Friday	Saturday
27	☐ Luke 19:28-48	☐ 20:1-19	☐ 20:20-38	☐ 20:39—21:4	☐ 21:5-27	☐ 21:28-38	☐ 22:1-20
28	☐ 22:21-38	☐ 22:39-54	☐ 22:55-71	☐ 23:1-43	☐ 23:44-56	☐ 24:1-12	☐ 24:13-35
29	☐ 24:36-53	☐ John 1:1-13	☐ 1:14-18	☐ 1:19-34	☐ 1:35-51	☐ 2:1-11	☐ 2:12-22
30	☐ 2:23—3:13	☐ 3:14-21	☐ 3:22-36	☐ 4:1-14	☐ 4:15-26	☐ 4:27-42	☐ 4:43-54
31	☐ 5:1-16	☐ 5:17-30	☐ 5:31-47	☐ 6:1-15	☐ 6:16-31	☐ 6:32-51	☐ 6:52-71
32	☐ 7:1-9	☐ 7:10-24	☐ 7:25-36	☐ 7:37-52	☐ 7:53—8:11	☐ 8:12-27	☐ 8:28-44
33	☐ 8:45-59	☐ 9:1-13	☐ 9:14-34	☐ 9:35—10:9	☐ 10:10-30	☐ 10:31—11:4	☐ 11:5-22
34	☐ 11:23-40	☐ 11:41-57	☐ 12:1-11	☐ 12:12-24	☐ 12:25-36	☐ 12:37-50	☐ 13:1-11
35	☐ 13:12-30	☐ 13:31-38	☐ 14:1-6	☐ 14:7-20	☐ 14:21-31	☐ 15:1-11	☐ 15:12-27
36	☐ 16:1-15	☐ 16:16-33	☐ 17:1-5	☐ 17:6-13	☐ 17:14-24	☐ 17:25—18:11	☐ 18:12-27
37	☐ 18:28-40	☐ 19:1-16	☐ 19:17-30	☐ 19:31-42	☐ 20:1-13	☐ 20:14-18	☐ 20:19-22
38	☐ 20:23-31	☐ 21:1-14	☐ 21:15-22	☐ 21:23-25	☐ Acts 1:1-8	☐ 1:9-14	☐ 1:15-26
39	☐ 2:1-13	☐ 2:14-21	☐ 2:22-36	☐ 2:37-41	☐ 2:42-47	☐ 3:1-18	☐ 3:19—4:22
40	☐ 4:23-37	☐ 5:1-16	☐ 5:17-32	☐ 5:33-42	☐ 6:1—7:1	☐ 7:2-29	☐ 7:30-60
41	☐ 8:1-13	☐ 8:14-25	☐ 8:26-40	☐ 9:1-19	☐ 9:20-43	☐ 10:1-16	☐ 10:17-33
42	☐ 10:34-48	☐ 11:1-18	☐ 11:19-30	☐ 12:1-25	☐ 13:1-12	☐ 13:13-43	☐ 13:44—14:5
43	☐ 14:6-28	☐ 15:1-12	☐ 15:13-34	☐ 15:35—16:5	☐ 16:6-18	☐ 16:19-40	☐ 17:1-18
44	☐ 17:19-34	☐ 18:1-17	☐ 18:18-28	☐ 19:1-20	☐ 19:21-41	☐ 20:1-12	☐ 20:13-38
45	☐ 21:1-14	☐ 21:15-26	☐ 21:27-40	☐ 22:1-21	☐ 22:22-29	☐ 22:30—23:11	☐ 23:12-15
46	☐ 23:16-30	☐ 23:31—24:21	☐ 24:22—25:5	☐ 25:6-27	☐ 26:1-13	☐ 26:14-32	☐ 27:1-26
47	☐ 27:27—28:10	☐ 28:11-22	☐ 28:23-31	☐ Rom 1:1-2	☐ 1:3-7	☐ 1:8-17	☐ 1:18-25
48	☐ 1:26—2:10	☐ 2:11-29	☐ 3:1-20	☐ 3:21-31	☐ 4:1-12	☐ 4:13-25	☐ 5:1-11
49	☐ 5:12-17	☐ 5:18—6:5	☐ 6:6-11	☐ 6:12-23	☐ 7:1-12	☐ 7:13-25	☐ 8:1-2
50	☐ 8:3-6	☐ 8:7-13	☐ 8:14-25	☐ 8:26-39	☐ 9:1-18	☐ 9:19—10:3	☐ 10:4-15
51	☐ 10:16—11:10	☐ 11:11-22	☐ 11:23-36	☐ 12:1-3	☐ 12:4-21	☐ 13:1-14	☐ 14:1-12
52	☐ 14:13-23	☐ 15:1-13	☐ 15:14-33	☐ 16:1-5	☐ 16:6-24	☐ 16:25-27	☐ 1 Cor 1:1-4

Reading Schedule for the Recovery Version of the New Testament with Footnotes

Wk.	Lord's Day	Monday	Tuesday	Wednesday	Thursday	Friday	Saturday
53	1 Cor 1:5-9	1:10-17	1:18-31	2:1-5	2:6-10	2:11-16	3:1-9
54	3:10-13	3:14-23	4:1-9	4:10-21	5:1-13	6:1-11	6:12-20
55	7:1-16	7:17-24	7:25-40	8:1-13	9:1-15	9:16-27	10:1-4
56	10:5-13	10:14-33	11:1-6	11:7-16	11:17-26	11:27-34	12:1-11
57	12:12-22	12:23-31	13:1-13	14:1-12	14:13-25	14:26-33	14:34-40
58	15:1-19	15:20-28	15:29-34	15:35-49	15:50-58	16:1-9	16:10-24
59	2 Cor 1:1-4	1:5-14	1:15-22	1:23—2:11	2:12-17	3:1-6	3:7-11
60	3:12-18	4:1-6	4:7-12	4:13-18	5:1-8	5:9-15	5:16-21
61	6:1-13	6:14—7:4	7:5-16	8:1-15	8:16-24	9:1-15	10:1-6
62	10:7-18	11:1-15	11:16-33	12:1-10	12:11-21	13:1-10	13:11-14
63	Gal 1:1-5	1:6-14	1:15-24	2:1-13	2:14-21	3:1-4	3:5-14
64	3:15-22	3:23-29	4:1-7	4:8-20	4:21-31	5:1-12	5:13-21
65	5:22-26	6:1-10	6:11-15	6:16-18	Eph 1:1-3	1:4-6	1:7-10
66	1:11-14	1:15-18	1:19-23	2:1-5	2:6-10	2:11-14	2:15-18
67	2:19-22	3:1-7	3:8-13	3:14-18	3:19-21	4:1-4	4:5-10
68	4:11-16	4:17-24	4:25-32	5:1-10	5:11-21	5:22-26	5:27-33
69	6:1-9	6:10-14	6:15-18	6:19-24	Phil 1:1-7	1:8-18	1:19-26
70	1:27—2:4	2:5-11	2:12-16	2:17-30	3:1-6	3:7-11	3:12-16
71	3:17-21	4:1-9	4:10-23	Col 1:1-8	1:9-13	1:14-23	1:24-29
72	2:1-7	2:8-15	2:16-23	3:1-4	3:5-15	3:16-25	4:1-18
73	1 Thes 1:1-3	1:4-10	2:1-12	2:13—3:5	3:6-13	4:1-10	4:11—5:11
74	5:12-28	2 Thes 1:1-12	2:1-17	3:1-18	1 Tim 1:1-2	1:3-4	1:5-14
75	1:15-20	2:1-7	2:8-15	3:1-13	3:14—4:5	4:6-16	5:1-25
76	6:1-10	6:11-21	2 Tim 1:1-10	1:11-18	2:1-15	2:16-26	3:1-13
77	3:14—4:8	4:9-22	Titus 1:1-4	1:5-16	2:1-15	3:1-8	3:9-15
78	Philem 1:1-11	1:12-25	Heb 1:1-2	1:3-5	1:6-14	2:1-9	2:10-18

Reading Schedule for the Recovery Version of the New Testament with Footnotes

Wk.	Lord's Day	Monday	Tuesday	Wednesday	Thursday	Friday	Saturday
79	Heb 3:1-6 ☐	3:7-19 ☐	4:1-9 ☐	4:10-13 ☐	4:14-16 ☐	5:1-10 ☐	5:11—6:3 ☐
80	6:4-8 ☐	6:9-20 ☐	7:1-10 ☐	7:11-28 ☐	8:1-6 ☐	8:7-13 ☐	9:1-4 ☐
81	9:5-14 ☐	9:15-28 ☐	10:1-18 ☐	10:19-28 ☐	10:29-39 ☐	11:1-6 ☐	11:7-19 ☐
82	11:20-31 ☐	11:32-40 ☐	12:1-2 ☐	12:3-13 ☐	12:14-17 ☐	12:18-26 ☐	12:27-29 ☐
83	13:1-7 ☐	13:8-12 ☐	13:13-15 ☐	13:16-25 ☐	James 1:1-8 ☐	1:9-18 ☐	1:19-27 ☐
84	2:1-13 ☐	2:14-26 ☐	3:1-18 ☐	4:1-10 ☐	4:11-17 ☐	5:1-12 ☐	5:13-20 ☐
85	1 Pet 1:1-2 ☐	1:3-4 ☐	1:5 ☐	1:6-9 ☐	1:10-12 ☐	1:13-17 ☐	1:18-25 ☐
86	2:1-3 ☐	2:4-8 ☐	2:9-17 ☐	2:18-25 ☐	3:1-13 ☐	3:14-22 ☐	4:1-6 ☐
87	4:7-16 ☐	4:17-19 ☐	5:1-4 ☐	5:5-9 ☐	5:10-14 ☐	2 Pet 1:1-2 ☐	1:3-4 ☐
88	1:5-8 ☐	1:9-11 ☐	1:12-18 ☐	1:19-21 ☐	2:1-3 ☐	2:4-11 ☐	2:12-22 ☐
89	3:1-6 ☐	3:7-9 ☐	3:10-12 ☐	3:13-15 ☐	3:16 ☐	3:17-18 ☐	1 John 1:1-2 ☐
90	1:3-4 ☐	1:5 ☐	1:6 ☐	1:7 ☐	1:8-10 ☐	2:1-2 ☐	2:3-11 ☐
91	2:12-14 ☐	2:15-19 ☐	2:20-23 ☐	2:24-27 ☐	2:28-29 ☐	3:1-5 ☐	3:6-10 ☐
92	3:11-18 ☐	3:19-24 ☐	4:1-6 ☐	4:7-11 ☐	4:12-15 ☐	4:16—5:3 ☐	5:4-13 ☐
93	5:14-17 ☐	5:18-21 ☐	2 John 1:1-3 ☐	1:4-9 ☐	1:10-13 ☐	3 John 1:1-6 ☐	1:7-14 ☐
94	Jude 1:1-4 ☐	1:5-10 ☐	1:11-19 ☐	1:20-25 ☐	Rev 1:1-3 ☐	1:4-6 ☐	1:7-11 ☐
95	1:12-13 ☐	1:14-16 ☐	1:17-20 ☐	2:1-6 ☐	2:7 ☐	2:8-9 ☐	2:10-11 ☐
96	2:12-14 ☐	2:15-17 ☐	2:18-23 ☐	2:24-29 ☐	3:1-3 ☐	3:4-6 ☐	3:7-9 ☐
97	3:10-13 ☐	3:14-18 ☐	3:19-22 ☐	4:1-5 ☐	4:6-7 ☐	4:8-11 ☐	5:1-6 ☐
98	5:7-14 ☐	6:1-8 ☐	6:9-17 ☐	7:1-8 ☐	7:9-17 ☐	8:1-6 ☐	8:7-12 ☐
99	8:13—9:11 ☐	9:12-21 ☐	10:1-4 ☐	10:5-11 ☐	11:1-4 ☐	11:5-14 ☐	11:15-19 ☐
100	12:1-4 ☐	12:5-9 ☐	12:10-18 ☐	13:1-10 ☐	13:11-18 ☐	14:1-5 ☐	14:6-12 ☐
101	14:13-20 ☐	15:1-8 ☐	16:1-12 ☐	16:13-21 ☐	17:1-6 ☐	17:7-18 ☐	18:1-8 ☐
102	18:9—19:4 ☐	19:5-10 ☐	19:11-16 ☐	19:17-21 ☐	20:1-6 ☐	20:7-10 ☐	20:11-15 ☐
103	21:1 ☐	21:2 ☐	21:3-8 ☐	21:9-13 ☐	21:14-18 ☐	21:19-21 ☐	21:22-27 ☐
104	22:1 ☐	22:2 ☐	22:3-11 ☐	22:12-15 ☐	22:16-17 ☐	22:18-21 ☐	

Week 1 — Day 4

Isa. 29:13 And the Lord said, Because this people draws near with their mouth, and with their lips they honor Me, yet they remove their heart far from Me, and their fear for Me is a commandment of men *merely* learned.

40:31 ...Those who wait on Jehovah will renew *their* strength; they will mount up with wings like eagles; they will run and will not faint; they will walk and will not become weary.

62:6-7 Upon your walls, O Jerusalem, I have appointed watchmen; all day and all night they will never keep silent. You who remind Jehovah, do not be dumb; and do not give Him quiet until He establishes and until He makes Jerusalem a praise in the earth.

Date _____

Week 1 — Day 5 — Today's verses

Isa. 60:7 All the flocks of Kedar will be gathered together to you; the rams of Nebaioth will minister to you; they will go up acceptably upon My altar, and I will beautify the house of My beauty.

13 The glory of Lebanon will come to you, the fir tree, the pine tree, and the box tree together, to beautify the place of My sanctuary; and I will make the place for My feet glorious.

Date _____

Week 1 — Day 3 — Today's verses

Isa. 40:3 The voice of one who cries in the wilderness: Make clear the way of Jehovah; make straight in the desert a highway for our God.

53:5 But He was wounded because of our transgressions; He was crushed because of our iniquities; the chastening for our peace was upon Him, and by His stripes we have been healed.

65:17 For I am now creating new heavens and a new earth, and the former things will not be remembered, nor will they come up in the heart.

Date _____

Week 1 — Today's verses

Isa. 4:2 In that day the Shoot of Jehovah will be beauty and glory, and the fruit of the earth, excellence and splendor, to those of Israel who have escaped.

7:14 Therefore the Lord Himself will give you a sign: Behold, the virgin will conceive and will bear a son, and she will call his name Immanuel.

32:2 And a man will be like a refuge from the wind and a covering from the tempest, like streams of water in a dry place, like the shadow of a massive rock in a wasted land.

Date _____

Week 1 — Day 2 — Today's verses

Isa. 66:12-13 For thus says Jehovah, I now am extending to her peace like a river, and the glory of the nations like an overflowing stream; and you will nurse, you will be carried on the hip, and you will be bounced on the knees. As one whom his mother comforts, so will I comfort you; and you will be comforted in Jerusalem.

54:5 For your Maker is your Husband; Jehovah of hosts is His name....

Date _____

Week 1 — Day 1 — Today's verses

Isa. 1:1 The vision of Isaiah the son of Amoz, which he saw concerning Judah and Jerusalem....

9:6-7 For a child is born to us, a Son is given to us; and the government is upon His shoulder; and His name will be called Wonderful Counselor, Mighty God, Eternal Father, Prince of Peace. To the increase of *His* government and to *His* peace there is no end, upon the throne of David and over His kingdom, to establish it and to uphold it in justice and righteousness from now to eternity. The zeal of Jehovah of hosts will accomplish this.

Date _____

Week 2 — Day 4

Isa. 64:8 But now, Jehovah, You are our Father; we are the clay; and You, our Potter; and all of us are the work of Your hand.

Isa. 54:5 For your Maker is your Husband; Jehovah of hosts is His name. And the Holy One of Israel is your Redeemer; He is called the God of all the earth.

_____
Date

Isa. 24:21 And in that day Jehovah will punish on high the host on high, and the kings of the earth on the earth.

Isa. 57:15 For thus says the high and exalted One, who inhabits eternity, whose name is Holy: I will dwell in the high and holy place, and with the contrite and lowly of spirit, to revive the spirit of the lowly and to revive the heart of the contrite.

Today's verses

_____
Date

Week 2 — Day 1   Today's verses

Exo. 3:14 And God said to Moses, I AM WHO I AM. And He said, Thus you shall say to the children of Israel, I AM has sent me to you.

John 8:58 Jesus said to them, Truly, truly, I say to you, Before Abraham came into being, I am.

_____
Date

Week 2 — Day 2   Today's verses

Isa. 5:16 But Jehovah of hosts is exalted in judgment, and the holy God shows Himself holy in righteousness.

Isa. 26:8 Indeed in the path of Your judgments, O Jehovah, we have waited for You. Your name, that is, Your memorial, is the desire of our soul.

_____
Date

Isa. 12:2-3 God is now my salvation; I will trust and not dread; for Jah Jehovah is my strength and song, and He has become my salvation. Therefore you will draw water with rejoicing from the springs of salvation.

_____
Date

Week 2 — Day 3   Today's verses

Isa. 45:15 Surely You are a God who hides Himself, O God of Israel, the Savior.

Isa. 40:5 Then the glory of Jehovah will be revealed, and all flesh will see it together, because the mouth of Jehovah has spoken.

_____
Date

Week 3 — Day 1

Today's verses

Acts
3:21 — Whom heaven must indeed receive until the times of the restoration of all things, of which God spoke through the mouth of His holy prophets from of old.

Isa.
65:18 — But rejoice and exult forever, in what I create, for I am now creating Jerusalem as an exultation and her people as a rejoicing.

_____
Date

Week 3 — Day 2

Today's verses

Isa.
65:17 — For I am now creating new heavens and a new earth, and the former things will not be remembered, nor will they come up in the heart.

Col.
1:17 — And He is before all things, and all things cohere in Him.

_____
Date

Week 3 — Day 3

Today's verses

Isa.
4:2 — In that day the Shoot of Jehovah will be beauty and glory, and the fruit of the earth, excellence and splendor, to those of Israel who have escaped.

7:14 — Therefore the Lord Himself will give you a sign: Behold, the virgin will conceive and will bear a son, and she will call his name Immanuel.

_____
Date

Week 3 — Day 4

Micah
5:2 — But you, O Bethlehem Ephrathah, so little to be among the thousands of Judah, from you there will come forth to Me He who is to be Ruler in Israel; and His goings forth are from ancient times, from the days of eternity.

Isa.
60:1 — Arise! Shine! For your light has come, and the glory of Jehovah has risen upon you.

Luke
1:42 — And she lifted up her voice with a loud cry and said, Blessed are you among women, and blessed is the fruit of your womb!

John
12:24 — Truly, truly, I say to you, Unless the grain of wheat falls into the ground and dies, it abides alone; but if it dies, it bears much fruit.

Isa.
4:5-6 — Jehovah will create over the entire region of Mount Zion and over all her convocations a cloud of smoke by day, and the brightness of a fiery flame by night; for the glory will be a canopy over all. And there will be a tabernacle as a daytime shade from the heat and as a refuge and a cover from storm and rain.

_____
Date

Week 4 — Day 1

Today's verses

Isa. 6:1 In the year that King Uzziah died I saw the Lord sitting on a high and lofty throne, and the train of His robe filled the temple.

6:5 ...My eyes have seen the King, Jehovah of hosts.

Rev. 22:1 ...He showed me a river of water of life, bright as crystal, proceeding out of the throne of God and of the Lamb...

Date _____

Week 4 — Day 2

Today's verses

Isa. 6:2-3 Seraphim hovered over Him, each having six wings: With two he covered his face, and with two he covered his feet, and with two he flew. And one called to the other, saying; Holy, holy, holy, Jehovah of hosts; the whole earth is filled with His glory.

John 12:41 These things said Isaiah because he saw His glory and spoke concerning Him.

Date _____

Week 4 — Day 3

Today's verses

Isa. 6:4-5 And the foundations of the threshold shook at the voice of him who called, and the house was filled with smoke. Then I said, Woe is me, for I am finished! For I am a man of unclean lips, and in the midst of a people of unclean lips I dwell; yet my eyes have seen the King, Jehovah of hosts.

Date _____

Week 4 — Day 4

Job 42:5-6 I had heard of You by the hearing of the ear, but now my eye has seen You; therefore I abhor myself, and I repent in dust and ashes.

Luke 5:8 And when Simon Peter saw this, he fell down at Jesus' knees, saying, Depart from me, for I am a sinful man, Lord.

Isa. 6:6-7 Then one of the seraphim flew to me with an ember in his hand, which he had taken from the altar with a pair of tongs. And he touched my mouth with it and said, Now that this has touched your lips, your iniquity is taken away, and your sin is purged.

4:4 When the Lord has washed away the filth of the daughters of Zion and has cleansed away the bloodstains of Jerusalem from her midst, by the judging Spirit and the burning Spirit.

Psa. 36:9 For with You is the fountain of life; in Your light we see light.

Today's verses

Isa. 6:8 Then I heard the voice of the Lord, saying, Whom shall I send? Who will go for Us? And I said, Here am I; send me.

John 17:21 That they all may be one; even as You, Father, are in Me and I in You, that they also may be in Us; that the world may believe that You have sent Me.

20:21-22 Then Jesus said to them again, Peace be to you; as the Father has sent Me, I also send you. And when He had said this, He breathed into them and said to them, Receive the Holy Spirit.

Date _____

Week 5 — Day 4

Isa. For a child is born to us, a Son is given to
9:6 us; and the government is upon His shoulder; and His name will be called Wonderful Counselor, Mighty God, Eternal Father, Prince of Peace.

Isa. To the increase of *His* government and to
9:7 *His* peace there is no end, upon the throne of David and over His kingdom, to establish it and to uphold it in justice and righteousness from now to eternity....

Eph. Being diligent to keep the oneness of the
4:3 Spirit in the uniting bond of peace.

Col. And let the peace of Christ arbitrate in
3:15 your hearts, to which also you were called in one Body; and be thankful.

Date

Week 5 — Day 1

Today's verses

Isa. Therefore the Lord Himself will give you a
7:14 sign: Behold, the virgin will conceive and will bear a son, and she will call his name Immanuel.

Luke ...The Holy Spirit will come upon you,
1:35 and the power of the Most High will overshadow you; therefore also the holy thing which is born will be called the Son of God.

Date

Week 5 — Day 2

Today's verses

Matt. ...Behold, an angel of the Lord appeared
1:20-21 to him in a dream, saying, Joseph, son of David, do not be afraid to take Mary your wife, for that which has been begotten in her is of the Holy Spirit. And she will bear a son, and you shall call His name Jesus, for *it is* He *who* will save His people from their sins.

Date

Week 5 — Day 3

Today's verses

Isa. For You are our Father, since Abraham
63:16 does not know us, and Israel does not acknowledge us. You, Jehovah, are our Father; our Redeemer from eternity is Your name.

Isa. But now, Jehovah, You are our Father; we
64:8 are the clay; and You, our Potter; and all of us are the work of Your hand.

Matt. "Behold, the virgin shall be with child
1:23 and shall bear a son, and they shall call His name Emmanuel" (which is translated, God with us).

18:20 For where there are two or three gathered into My name, there am I in their midst.

2 Tim. The Lord be with your spirit. Grace be
4:22 with you.

Date

Week 6 — Day 4

Today's verses

Isa. 42:6-7   I am Jehovah; I have called You in righteousness; I have held You by the hand; I have kept You and I have given You as a covenant for the people, as a light for the nations; to open the eyes of the blind, to bring the prisoner out from the prison, those who dwell in darkness from the prison house.

_____
Date

Week 6 — Day 5

Today's verses

Eph. 5:8-9   For you were once darkness but are now light in the Lord; walk as children of light (for the fruit of the light *consists* in all goodness and righteousness and truth).

Matt. 5:14   You are the light of the world. It is impossible for a city situated upon a mountain to be hidden.

Rev. 21:23-24   And the city has no need of the sun or of the moon that they should shine in it, for the glory of God illumined it, and its lamp is the Lamb. And the nations will walk by its light…

_____
Date

Week 6 — Day 1

Today's verses

John 8:12   …Jesus spoke to them, saying, I am the light of the world; he who follows Me shall by no means walk in darkness, but shall have the light of life.

1:4   In Him was life, and the life was the light of men.

_____
Date

Week 6 — Day 2

Today's verses

Isa. 9:2   The people who walked in the darkness have seen a great light; upon those who dwell in the land of the shadow of death light has shined.

4   For You break the yoke of their burden and the staff on their shoulder, the rod of their oppressor, as in the day of Midian.

_____
Date

Week 6 — Day 3

Today's verses

John 12:46   I have come as a light into the world, that everyone who believes into Me would not remain in darkness.

Matt. 4:19-20   And He said to them, Come after Me, and I will make you fishers of men. And immediately leaving the nets, they followed Him.

_____
Date